Essential Histories

The Spanish Civil War

1936–1939

Essential Histories

The Spanish Civil War

1936–1939

Francis Lannon

First published in Great Britain in 2002 by Osprey Publishing,
Midland House, West Way, Botley, Oxford OX2 0PH, UK
443 Park Avenue South, New York, NY 10016, USA
Email: info@ospreypublishing.com

ISBN-13 : 978-1-84176-369-9
Typeset in Monotype Gill Sans and ITC Stone Serif

CIP Data for this publication is available from the British Library
Design: Ken Vail Graphic Design, Cambridge, UK
Cartography by The Map Studio
Index by Alison Worthington
Picture research by Image Select International
Origination by PPS Grasmere Ltd., Leeds, UK
Printed in China through Bookbuilders

08 09 10 11 12   15 14 13 12 11 10 9 8 7 6

For a complete list of titles available from Osprey Publishing
please contact:

NORTH AMERICA
Osprey Direct, C/o Random House Distribution Center,
400 Hahn Road, Westminster, MD 21157
E-mail: info@ospreydirect.com

ALL OTHER REGIONS
Osprey Direct UK, P.O. Box 140, Wellingborough,
Northants, NN8 2FA, UK
E-mail: info@ospreydirect.co.uk

www.ospreypublishing.com

Contents

Introduction

The Spanish Civil War of 1936–39 was a class war, and a culture war. Competing visions of Spanish identity were superimposed on a bitter struggle over material resources, as the defenders of property, religion and tradition took up arms against a Republican government committed to social reform, devolution and secularisation. Directly or indirectly, the conflict caused about half a million deaths in a population of 24 million.

The war began in the middle of July 1936, when a group of generals attempted a military coup against the democratically constituted government of the Second Spanish Republic. Their plan was to co-ordinate a number of simultaneous risings in different parts of the country. If they had succeeded, the military would have supplanted civilian politicians and taken over government, as General Miguel Primo de Rivera had done in 1923. If they had failed everywhere, they would have been tried for military rebellion, as had already happened to one of their number, General José Sanjurjo, in 1932.

Instead, they succeeded in some parts of Spain, including – fatefully – Spanish Morocco, and failed in others, including – equally fatefully – the capital city of Madrid and the industrial powerhouses of Barcelona and Bilbao. Spain was split in two, and a harsh civil war was fought for nearly three years until, at the end of March 1939, the rebel generals completed their slow territorial conquest of the country by eventually taking the major prize that had eluded them throughout the war, Madrid itself.

The Second Republic, which had been inaugurated only in 1931, was definitively replaced by the dictatorship of General Francisco Franco, which was to last until his death in November 1975. It would, therefore, be difficult to exaggerate the significance of the civil war, both for those Spaniards who had hoped the Republic would usher in an unprecedented era of social justice and modernisation, and for others who regarded it as a revolutionary and irreligious assault on Spanish tradition. Winning the war was the precondition for shaping the future of Spain, and losing it meant political, economic, cultural and even physical exclusion from that process. The postwar repression removed tens of thousands of opponents of the new regime by execution, and more by imprisonment. Others fled into exile. The dictatorship was determined to make the peace a continuation of the war by other means. Postwar Spain would be Franco's Spain.

From the very beginning, however, this civil war also attracted international attention and foreign involvement. Governments, political parties, trade unions, churches and private citizens across Europe and even beyond, recognised that the conflict in Spain, however domestic its origins, was crucially important for them. Suddenly Spain seemed for thousands who had never been there, and who had never paid it much attention before, the centre of the world. And in a sense it was, because the conflict was ideological as well as political and military. Making the social revolution or breaking it, defending religion or destroying it, stopping fascism or joining it, saving democracy or overturning it – these were issues that were significant far beyond Spain's frontiers.

The options were either to participate and influence the outcome both in Spain and more widely, or to stay out and seek to prevent the escalation of the Spanish conflict into a European war. Hitler, Mussolini and Stalin all took the first option, with the Nazi

'Rise up against the Italian invasion of Spain'. Republican poster from the Civil War. The Republicans claimed that they were the true patriots, defending Spanish democracy against Nazi and Fascist invaders fighting with Franco. But the Republicans came to rely on Soviet help as much as Franco did on Germany and Italy. (Author's collection)

and Fascist regimes supporting Franco, and the Soviet Union supporting the Republic – with momentous consequences for the war in Spain. So too did volunteers from dozens of countries who joined the International Brigades and defended the Republic, and a small number, mainly from Ireland, who briefly fought on the other side. Britain and France adopted the second option and pursued a policy of non-intervention aimed at limiting the conflict by making arms sales to Spain illegal.

Foreign intervention and international restrictions on arms purchases changed the military balance of the war at several stages. The internationalising of the war also affected the exercise of power behind the lines. On Franco's side, the evidence of statements by generals at the time of the July rising reveals that their chief pre-occupations were national unity, and law and order. They wanted to end the Republic's experiment with devolution, and to curb the waves of street violence, land occupations and strikes that seemed to be swelling out of control. Beyond these aims, individual generals had a variety of political objectives, ranging from

the restoration of the monarchy, which had collapsed in 1931, or the establishment of an alternative and more illiberal monarchical line in Carlism, to the promotion of the Spanish fascist movement, the Falange, and even the continuation of the Republic, but under a different constitution.

By the end of the war, monarchists, fascists and law-and-order Republicans had learned to bow to Franco's supremacy as his personal dictatorship was consolidated. Moreover, the Catholic Church emerged as a particularly notable beneficiary of the victory of the rebel generals, most of whom had not had this result in mind at all when embarking on their attempted coup.

On the Republican side, the changes wrought during the war were even more dramatic. The Communist party had swollen from a small presence to become the dominant political force, and an anti-revolutionary force at that, eclipsing those – the Anarchists, many Socialists and some anti-Stalinist Communists – for whom the Republic had come to mean social revolution or nothing. Democrats who wanted to secure the continuation of the parliamentary Republic as it was in the early summer of 1936 saw that possibility fade away under the pressures of war, then social revolution, then increasing reliance on the Soviet Union. Not all of those who took up arms to defend the Republic in 1936 were convinced that it was worth fighting for in 1939. And among the victors, some were disillusioned that their efforts resulted in a military dictatorship.

'The National Side'. Republican Civil War poster. The Republican Ministry of Propaganda mocks Franco's claim that his side, 'the Nationals' or 'the Nationalists', represented the true Spain, by depicting the foreign forces - big business, Nazis, Fascists, international Catholicism, Moroccan troops - which supported him. (Author's collection)

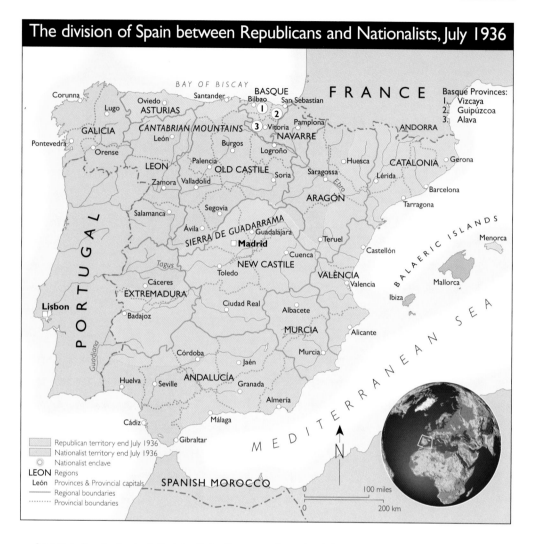

The division of Spain between Republicans and Nationalists, July 1936

Soviet policy in Spain failed, both in the defeat of the Republic and in Stalin's inability to draw Britain and France into an anti-Nazi alliance. Germany and Italy gained a very sympathetic Spanish regime, but not one that actively joined a fascist front when war broke out in Europe in September 1939. Meanwhile, British and French policy not only proved unable to prevent armed intervention in Spain by three major powers, but also left Britain and France isolated when the Soviet Union despaired of them and in August 1939 did the unthinkable and entered a non-aggression pact with Nazi Germany. The Spanish Civil War was not a rehearsal for the Second World War, but it significantly affected the balance of forces when that war began. In Spain itself, the rebels of 1936 became the victors, and with them, counter-revolution triumphed.

Chronology

1931   14 April Second Spanish Republic proclaimed
        May Churches burned in Madrid
        December Constitution of the Republic approved
1933   November Spanish right wins general election
1934   October Three CEDA ministers join the government
        October Attempted revolution
1936   February Popular Front wins general election
        13 July Calvo Sotelo killed
        17 July Military rising against Republic starts in Morocco
        18 July Military rising in several parts of mainland Spain
        19 July Rising defeated in Madrid and Barcelona; social revolution breaks out in Republican Spain
        27 July German and Italian planes begin airlifting the Army of Africa from Morocco to southern Spain
        August Britain and France begin policy of non-intervention
        14 August Yagüe's troops capture Badajoz from Republic
        4 September Largo Caballero forms new Republican government
        9 September Non-Intervention Committee established in London
        13 September San Sebastián taken by Nationalists
        27 September Relief of the siege of the Alcázar in Toledo
        October Republic incorporates militias into new Popular Army
        1 October Franco becomes head of Nationalist government and supreme military commander
        7 October Aguirre forms Basque government of Euzkadi
        29 October Soviet intervention begins; German and Italian planes bomb Madrid
        6 November Republican government leaves Madrid for Valencia
        8 November First involvement of the International Brigade, in Madrid
        20 November José Antonio Primo de Rivera executed in Alicante
        23 November Nationalists abandon attempt to take Madrid
        December Nationalist offensive on Madrid–Corunna road
1937   February Battle of Jarama
        8 February Fall of Málaga to the Nationalists
        March Battle of Guadalajara
        April Franco unites Carlists, Fascists and Monarchists in one political movement
        26 April Condor Legion bombs and destroys Guernica
        2–6 May Fighting between Republican advocates and opponents of revolution in Barcelona
        15 May Fall of Largo Caballero
        17 May Negrín forms new government
        19 June Fall of Bilbao to the Nationalists
        July Republic's offensive at Brunete
        August Council of Aragón dissolved and agrarian collectives ended
        24 August Start of Republican offensive at Saragossa; battle for Blechite
        31 October Republican government moved from Valencia to Barcelona
        December Republican offensive at Teruel, followed by Nationalist counter-offensive
1938   22 February Nationalists retake Teruel

March Air bombardment of Barcelona
14 April Nationalists reach
Mediterranean at Vinaroz, splitting
Republic in two
25 July Republican army crosses the
Ebro in major offensive
November Republican army beaten
back across the Ebro
15 November Farewell parade of
International Brigades in Barcelona
1939 **26 January** Nationalists take
Barcelona

February 400,000 Republican
refugees cross Catalan border into
France
27 February Britain and France
recognise Franco's government
28 February Azaña resigns the
Presidency of the Republic
5 March Casado sets up National
Defence Council in Madrid
28 March Nationalists enter Madrid
1 April Franco announces the end of
the war

The democratic experiment

The Spanish Civil War began when army officers rose against the Second Republic in July 1936. But the potential for conflict was rooted in long-term, structural imbalances in Spanish society and the economy, and in the failure of successive regimes to construct a state system that enjoyed undisputed legitimacy. Political power had traditionally been concentrated in the hands of a small elite, who had not learned the trick of moderate reform aimed at co-opting the masses. On their great estates in south and west Spain, landowners faced a restive population of agricultural labourers and poor tenants, trapped by the lack of alternative employment opportunities. Their living standards were miserable, many were unemployed for parts of each year, and literacy levels in some areas were as low as 20 per cent. The state offered them little beyond the repressive presence of the Civil Guard, the militarised police force founded in the 1840s to keep order in the countryside.

Industrial workers struggled with low wages, unregulated working conditions, poor housing and virtually no social welfare provision. Moreover, the rapidly expanding working-class areas of cities like Barcelona, Bilbao and Madrid lacked an adequate urban infrastructure in the form of decent sanitation, paving and lighting, making them a danger to health. In both town and country, there were neither enough schools to provide even elementary education for all, nor basic medical services. The infant mortality rate among the poor remained depressingly high.

It was no wonder that the propertyless masses of Spain, and the political modernisers who championed them, wanted to redress the imbalance of power and resources, and hailed the Second Republic as the great opportunity to do so. At the same time, many conservatives, including very modest property-owners as well as the wealthy, feared that once the balance began to shift, revolutionary claims for redistribution of wealth would overwhelm them.

In these circumstances, the proclamation of the Second Republic on 14 April 1931 was an extraordinary turning point in Spanish history. The Bourbon monarchy, first established in Spain back in 1715 at the end of the War of the Spanish Succession, had been overturned before, first by Napoleon in 1808, and then by disillusioned politicians and generals in 1868. Both times it had been restored. Since the end of the 19th century, however, it had experienced several major crises. In 1898, the calamitous defeat in war by the United States and the loss of Cuba, Puerto Rico and the Philippines virtually spelled the end of a once-great empire. Military disasters in the fragment of empire that remained, in north Africa, in the period 1909–22, were accompanied by political instability and domestic unrest. In 1923 General Primo de Rivera seized power, under the king, and suspended the constitution; the monarchy's legitimacy was fatally undermined.

Then in 1931, for the first time, popular opinion declared against the crown in a way that could be quantified, at the ballot box. The elections of 12 April 1931 were merely municipal elections, designed as the first step back to constitutional normality. Nationwide, more pro-monarchist than anti-monarchist candidates were successful. But it was recognised, not least by King Alfonso XIII himself, that these local elections were a plebiscite, and that the results which mattered were those in the big cities and provincial capitals, far from the control of traditional elites whose influence often falsified results in rural Spain. The free voice of urban Spain was

Civil Guards. The Civil Guards were a militarised police force founded in the 1840s to keep order, first in the countryside, and then in towns and cities. They were a widely feared repressive force. Here they are shown in a poor district of Barcelona, near architect Antoní Gaudí's famous Sagrada Familia church. (Topham Picturepoint)

loudly Republican or Socialist, and the king, after consultation with political and military advisers, left the country.

If Alfonso had ignored the election results, or tried to impose martial law, he might have provoked revolution or civil war in 1931. Faced with this prospect, and the collapse of support even among erstwhile monarchists, he chose instead to depart. On 14 April the Republic was proclaimed amid scenes of euphoric jubilation in Madrid. An era was over, and those who welcomed the Republic as the beginning of a new age of genuine democracy and social justice were confident that – unlike the first Republic that had lasted only a year back in 1873–74 – it would stand and deliver. But others who were willing, with whatever misgivings, to

give it a chance in 1931 took up arms against it only five years later. Their action in July 1936 plunged Spain into war. But over-ambitious Republican policies contributed greatly to their alienation, and were also a major cause of the civil war of 1936–39.

What did the Republic represent to the Spanish population in the heady days of April 1931? Crucially, it represented not just a change of regime, but a turning upside-down of established values and hierarchies. The Republic had enormous symbolic potency. Its name immediately suggested not just the end of the monarchy, but also a challenge to the policies and institutions historically associated with it. One example was the insistent centralisation that had been one of the hallmarks of the Bourbon

The New York Times announces the end of the Bourbon monarchy in Spain. After municipal elections showed that there was little popular support for the monarchy, King Alfonso XIII left Spain, and on 14 April 1931 the Second Republic was proclaimed. It was a peaceful transition, but the new Republic faced daunting problems. (Aisa)

project since the early 18th century. So obvious was this implication of the word 'Republic' that, in the very first days, its government had to restrain exuberant Catalan nationalists from establishing a separate Catalan Republic. Devolution for Catalonia and potentially for the other historic regions of the Basque country and Galicia was inescapable, and was soon written into the new constitution.

Similarly, no one expected the Republic to continue the church–state alliance that had existed between Catholicism and the crown. The separation of church and state and the introduction of religious freedom were inevitable concomitants of the historic turn to Republicanism. Many of the bishops feared something worse, namely an active attempt to secularise Spanish society and culture, and to limit the freedom of action of the church. Traditional religious privileges were clearly under threat; the question was how far the assault would go.

If bishops were wary and pessimistic, so too were many of the generals. Monarchy had been identified historically with religion and empire. But the Republic symbolised change and modernisation. It would surely rationalise an oversized army left over from empire. Moreover, it was bound to assert the supremacy of civil authority over military as well as religious claims to embody national identity.

In social and economic matters too, 'Republic' was not a neutral term. It implied a shift in public policy in favour of the working masses and the poor. Land reform, jobs, improved wages and better public provision for health and particularly education were essential items on the Republican agenda. It was the promise, however implicit, of work, schools and access to a better life that brought working men to the voting booths to topple the toffs of the old regime. The prospect of social

A symbolic representation of the Second Spanish Republic. The female figure wears classical dress, the revolutionary bonnet of the French revolutionaries of 1789, and carries an olive branch of peace. The Republic positioned itself symbolically within a long European tradition. (Topham Pictuepoint)

justice as well as political renewal turned the proclamation of the Republic into a mass celebration. But the economic circumstances of the great depression cast a huge question mark over what any government would actually be able to achieve for the rural and urban working classes.

'Republic' was a code that Spaniards knew how to read. The old order had been monarchist, centralist, Catholic, imbued with the values of empire and arms, and run by and largely for the social and economic elites. The new order, therefore, was not merely a political system without a king. The Republic meant, for those who cheered its arrival, a democratic, civilian, secular order, in which the centre would have to be responsive to the periphery, and the top to the bottom. For those who were sceptical or hostile, it meant the abandonment of tradition, and a threat to stability, property and national unity. Within days of the Republic's proclamation, the Catholic newspaper *El Debate* was trying to rally its readers under the slogan 'Religion, Fatherland, Order, Family and Property'. The outlines of the two sides in the civil war of 1936–39 were already visible, even though war itself was far from inevitable.

The weight of popular expectation on the new Republic was enormous. Although the monarchy had collapsed, the institutions and social sectors long identified with it – church, army, landlords, the barons of finance and industry – were all still in place. Except in politics, there had been no revolution. Instead, the Republic now set out to instigate and manage a transformation of Spanish society by democratic methods, and in exceptionally difficult economic circumstances, without provoking a backlash of angry reaction. This was a task that no one knew how to accomplish. To make matters worse, there was no consensus among those within the Republican camp about what kind and degree of transformation was desirable. Disagreement over this weakened and divided the Republic from its inception through to the last days of the civil war in 1939.

The men who suddenly found themselves forming the Provisional Government of Spain had previously pledged themselves to the overthrow of the monarchy, in an agreement called the San Sebastián pact. But they represented a wide range of different views about what should happen next. The Prime Minister and later the first President of the Republic, Niceto Alcalá-Zamora, was a Catholic, and a convert from monarchism, as was Miguel Maura, Minister of the Interior. For them, the Republic was itself a revolution and they saw no need for any other, although they recognised the urgency of social reform. The leader of the Radical party, Alejandro Lerroux, was famous for the demagogic anti-clericalism of his youth, but had no desire to see a social revolution overthrow property.

Manuel Azaña, the single most important politician in the entire Republic, Minister for War in the Provisional Government, then Prime Minister, and eventually the second President, was a secularising intellectual who was offended by the public role and educational monopoly of the Catholic Church in Spain. He wanted the Second Spanish Republic to emulate the pre-1914 Third French Republic, make secular schooling free and compulsory, and construct a non-religious basis for national culture and citizenship. For Azaña, as for many on the left, this was an essential part of the necessary updating and Europeanising of Spain.

Devolution was the overwhelming priority for Catalan Republicans who had one representative in the government. The three Socialists, Indalecio Prieto (Finance Minister) the trade unionist Francisco Largo Caballero (Minister of Labour) and Fernando de los Ríos (Minister of Justice), wanted to alleviate the worst hardships of the urban and rural poor. They also wanted to help consolidate the 'bourgeois' Republic. The socialisation of production and distribution would have to wait for a later stage. Not all their followers were so patient.

In the spring and summer of 1931, the Provisional Government held supreme authority in Spain while preparations were made for general elections in June to create a Constituent Assembly that met in July. The government acted quickly to aid the labouring masses, especially in agriculture. Largo Caballero issued decrees in April through to early July, introducing the eight-hour day, establishing joint arbitration committees between rural employers and labourers, and preventing landowners from importing cheap labour from outside their own immediate area, by requiring them to employ agricultural labourers from within it first.

Swift action was also taken on other fronts. The government agreed that,

Manuel Azaña, photographed in May 1936, when he was the President of the Spanish Republic. He had earlier been Minister for War, and Prime Minister. Once the rising against the Republic began in July 1936, he was pessimistic about the Republic's chances of victory. (Topham Picturepoint)

although the June elections would be held on the existing basis of adult male suffrage, women would nonetheless be eligible for election as deputies, for the first time in Spanish history. Minister of War, Azaña immediately tackled what he regarded as the most pressing of army problems, the excessive number of officers, in a decree of 25 April offering all officers immediate retirement on full pay, with a threat that retirements would be forced if it proved necessary. It did not: retirement requests flowed in. The officer corps was cut by 40 per cent to between 12,000 and 13,000 in a few months. This success was modified by two elements: no political criteria were used, so there was no guarantee that the officers who stayed were pro-Republican; and many were offended that such a radical measure had been imposed by decree. Meanwhile, religious liberty was declared and Catholic images were removed from state schoolrooms. The Catholic Minister of the Interior, Miguel Maura, even took action against the Cardinal Archbishop of Toledo, Pedro Segura, insisting he leave Spain after provocatively anti-Republican behaviour.

In all of these ways, the reforming agenda of the new regime was apparent. But internal divisions had already become visible over another matter concerning religion. On Sunday, 10 May 1931, monarchist youths played the royal anthem from their new centre on Alcalá street in Madrid. Angry crowds gathered to protest. Civil Guards, unable to control the crowd, fired, and killed two people. The next day, various groups set fire to churches and convents in the capital, forcing nuns to flee as their accommodation went up in flames, and leaving a trail of burnt-out buildings.

It was obvious that the government could have smothered the flames and the lawlessness swiftly by calling out the Civil Guard. But to Maura's fury, it refused to do so, on the specious grounds that, as Azaña – Minister for War – unwisely remarked, 'all the convents in Madrid are not worth the life of one Republican'. It delayed before restoring order. The next day, the attacks were repeated elsewhere, especially in Málaga. Many ordinary Catholics concluded that the new state would not respect their religion or protect property.

The June elections were a triumph for the left and a disaster for conservatives, who were disorganised after the collapse of the monarchy. No one party held a majority in the assembly, but the Spanish Socialist Workers' Party (the PSOE) was the largest, with 117 deputies. The PSOE, founded in 1879, was backed by the Socialist trade unions (the UGT), and probably on this occasion by the votes of the large Anarchist movement as well, which as a matter of principle did not form a political party of its own, or put up representatives for election.

The Anarchist unions (the CNT), which were strong in the rural south and in the largest manufacturing concentration in Spain, round Barcelona, remained a powerful extra-parliamentary presence committed to the social ownership of property and production, to social egalitarianism and to the abolition of religion. Their revolutionary agenda put constant pressure on the Socialists, and on the Republic as a whole. From the Anarchists' point of view, the Republic was on trial, and would be judged on its ability to deliver a new social order.

To the right of the Socialists stood the Radical Socialists with 59 deputies, and Lerroux's Radicals with 89. Azaña's Republican Action party, like the conservative Catholic Republicanism of Alcalá-Zamora and Miguel Maura, lacked a mass following, and each of them gained only 27 seats. Spain's subsequent history in the 1930s might have been different if there had been a strong centre to hold the balance between left and right, but this was never the case. To the right of the Catholic Republicans stood two sets of monarchists, the Alfonsists, who wanted to restore Alfonso XIII to his throne, and the Carlists, who supported a rival branch of the royal family and a more traditionalist kind of monarchy. For both, the Republic always lacked legitimacy.

An early sign of polarisation was the outright repudiation by the new parliament, as soon as it met on 14 July 1931, of a constitutional draft prepared by a commission under a reformist Catholic lawyer, Angel Ossorio y Gallardo. This draft separated church and state, established religious liberty and recognised popular sovereignty. It was not enough. Instead, a new commission under the presidency of the Socialist lawyer Luis Jiménez de Asúa produced a radical constitutional draft for 'a Republic of workers of all classes'. When the Constituent Assembly approved an amended draft on 9 December 1931, it created a secular democratic system based on equal rights for all citizens, with provision for regional autonomy. It introduced female suffrage, civil marriage and divorce. To the dismay of property-owners great and small, it permitted the state to expropriate private property, with compensation, for reasons of broader social utility. It also established free, obligatory, secular education for all, dissolved the Jesuits, and banned the religious communities of nuns, priests and brothers from teaching even in private schools. Jiménez's unamended draft would have dissolved all the religious orders outright.

Alcalá-Zamora and Maura resigned from the government in October 1931 when the revised article 26, on religion, was passed. Even though Alcalá-Zamora became the first President of the Republic after the whole constitution was approved, the articles on property and religion, with their exaltation of state power and their disregard for civil rights, virtually destroyed any prospect there had been for the development of a Catholic, conservative, Republicanism.

With this divisive constitution in force, Azaña became Prime Minister and chose to govern in coalition with the Socialists rather than the Radicals. Parliament bitterly debated through 1932 and 1933 a series of laws to implement the constitutional measures on devolution, land, education, civil marriage and divorce, and the church. An attempted coup by General Sanjurjo in August 1932 signalled the depth of discontent in some

quarters, but failed. However, when a mass party of the right was organised in February 1933, in the shape of the CEDA (the Spanish Confederation of Autonomous Right-Wing Groups), its programme inevitably included the defence of Catholicism, order, property and the family. Its leader, José María Gil Robles, refused to commit the party to loyalty to the Republic.

For Gil Robles, and of course for the monarchists, the Republic had already gone much too far in its first two years. He was determined to reverse its direction. However, for many of its original supporters, the Republic had not gone far enough. A Catalan autonomy statute was passed in the summer of 1932, but the process for autonomy in the Basque country was moving very slowly. The 1932 Agrarian Reform Law opened the way for the redistribution of land, but in fact very little land was expropriated, and only about 12,000 landless families were settled.

The growth of unrest

Labour radicalisation was evident in strikes and unrest in both industry and agriculture. Indeed, the Republican–Socialist coalition repressed strikes and imposed law and order by the same rough methods as previous governments. An Anarchist general strike in the summer of 1931 was crushed by the army, leaving 30 people dead. In the village of Castilblanco, in Badajoz province, in Extremadura, a demonstration by rural workers who were members of the Socialist agricultural union the FNTT (National Federation of Landworkers), at the end of December 1931, was broken up by the Civil Guard with gunfire, killing one of the demonstrators and wounding two others. In fury, the crowd turned on the four Civil Guards and lynched them. A national general strike called by the Anarchist unions at the end of January 1932 was put down severely. In January 1933, an Anarchist revolutionary rising was crushed in several places. But in the village of Casas Viejas, in Cádiz province, local Anarchists held out and were surrounded by Guards. They set fire to a shack at the centre of resistance, and shot anyone trying to escape.

The government was blamed by the right for the extent of disorder, and by the left for brutal repression. To strikers and demonstrators, the state – in its visible manifestation, the forces of law and order – looked just the same as it had always done. To conservatives, the government looked incompetent. It was a supporter of the Republic, not one of its foes, who described it in 1933 as a regime of 'blood, mud, and tears'. During 1933 the Socialist party became increasingly disillusioned, and the Republican–Socialist alliance disintegrated. President Alcalá-Zamora's attempts to have the Radicals govern without Azaña or the Socialists failed, and he called general elections for November 1933. The first *bienio* was over.

At the time of the 1933 election campaign, Mussolini had been in power in Italy for over 10 years, and Hitler's first 10 months in power in Germany had been enough to show that there too, democracy, free speech and the right to association were things of the past. José María Gil Robles, leader of the CEDA, had recently returned from an enthusiastic visit to the Nuremberg rally, and incorporated Nazi rhetoric and style into his election campaign. He spoke of the new state that must emerge, and argued that democracy was useful only if it delivered anti-Marxist policies and a 'totalitarian polity'. His programme was the repeal of the laws on religion and property of the first *bienio*, and the revision of the constitution.

On this basis, the CEDA entered an electoral coalition with monarchists, and in some areas with Radicals. In an electoral system that gave 80 per cent of the seats in each province to the party or coalition with a majority of the votes, that strategy was wise. By contrast, Socialists and left Republicans faced the electorate separately, and paid the price for their mutual disaffection. The CEDA won 115 seats, the Radicals 104, but the Socialists dropped from 117 to 58, while Radical Socialists and Azaña's Republicans all but disappeared. The Socialist disaster was compounded by the massive abstention of disillusioned Anarchists. In terms of parliamentary seats, even if not in numbers of votes, the political pendulum had swung from left to right.

For almost a year, governments of Alejandro Lerroux's Radicals, backed in parliament by the CEDA, ruled Spain. They systematically unpicked the agrarian and social legislation of the Republican–Socialist coalition. Since that had largely been targeted at the agricultural south, this was also where the effects of political change were most obvious, in falling wages, enhanced employer power and the lapse of land redistribution. Part of the price for CEDA support of the Radicals was the repeal, the suspension or sometimes simply the non-implementation of legislation on religion.

The Radical party, which in its wilder days in the early 1900s had been ferociously anti-clerical, now feared that the assault on Catholicism was part of a wider social revolution against property and the family, which had to be stopped. In June 1934, the government met a strike by the Socialist landworkers' union (FNTT) with force. Also that summer, it became locked in conflict with the left-wing autonomous government of Catalonia, over agricultural tenancies.

Gil Robles demanded more, and in October 1934 a new Radical government, headed by Lerroux, was formed, which contained three CEDA ministers, in the key ministries of Labour, Agriculture and Justice. For many on the left, this was the end of the Republic in any meaningful sense. Socialists who had preached moderation in 1931 and 1932, in extremely provoking circumstances, decided that the CEDA in government was the beginning of a fascist takeover, and determined on a revolution for which they and their allies had made few preparations.

Sanjurjo's attempted coup in 1932 had been an early sign of right-wing impatience with democracy. Another followed in October 1933, when José Antonio Primo de Rivera, son of the 1920s dictator, formed the Spanish fascist party, the Falange, and in

February 1934 united it with another group of the extreme right, the JONS. Meanwhile, the Carlists began training young volunteers, the *requetés*, in their stronghold in Navarre.

It was against this background that the disenchantment of the left with the parliamentary Republic exploded in the strikes and risings of October 1934. Largo Caballero had abandoned reformism for revolution, and even Indalecio Prieto capitulated. Socialists rose against the Republic, in Madrid with a few members of the small Communist party, and in Barcelona with Catalan left Republicans who proclaimed an independent Catalonia. These efforts were suppressed immediately, as were strikes elsewhere in Spain.

Only in the northern mining area of Asturias had the revolution been seriously prepared. Local alliances of Socialists, Anarchists and Communists proclaimed a Socialist republic, and had the arms to create it. Revolutionary committees took over towns and villages, many buildings were destroyed, and some Civil Guards, industrialists and priests were killed. Faced with revolutionary soviets, the government clearly had to assert its authority and regain control. Prime Minister Lerroux did so by calling in General Francisco Franco, the Spanish Foreign Legion and Moroccan troops, all of them formed in the colonial wars in Morocco. Oviedo and Gijón were retaken swiftly, while several more days were needed to subdue mining villages one by one.

The death toll was high, not just during the fighting but also in the brutal military repression that followed. About a thousand workers were killed in the pacification, and many thousands of political prisoners were taken in Asturias and elsewhere in Spain, including Largo Caballero, who was certainly involved in the rising, and Azaña, who was not. Amnesty for these prisoners became the rallying call of the Spanish left, as it surveyed the devastation and pondered what to do next.

Chastened by the extremes of revolutionary militancy among the miners, and the severity of the repression, Prieto edged back towards the aim of regaining political control of parliament. But for many at grassroots level, October 1934 confirmed that parliamentary democracy was a lost cause. Meanwhile the vision of revolution in action added to the growing conviction on the right that the 'Bolshevik' danger could only be overcome by force. If the blurred outlines of civil war had already been visible in 1931, they were now hard to ignore.

Of the 20 death penalties handed down after October, all but two were commuted. But Gil Robles was appointed Minister for War. Catalan autonomy was suspended. Projects for a revised land reform were abandoned. When the governing Radical party collapsed in a corruption scandal in 1935, Alcalá-Zamora chose to call new elections rather than appoint Gil Robles head of government. The second, 'black' *bienio* followed its predecessor into history. Senior generals considered seizing power immediately, but drew back. General elections were scheduled for 16 February 1936. The outbreak of civil war was only five months away.

From the Popular Front to Civil War

In the elections of February 1936, the options were starkly polarised. Conservatives associated the left with revolution, while the left regarded their opponents as reactionary and possibly fascist. José María Gil Robles hoped to gain power for the CEDA, in order to revise the Republic's constitution and make it more acceptable to the right. He wanted an outright majority in parliament, which would leave President Alcalá-Zamora no choice but to appoint him Prime Minister. Opponents feared he would emulate Hitler's use of the Chancellorship in Germany or Dollfuss's in Austria, to dismantle democracy from within.

In any case, an outright majority was difficult to achieve other than in an electoral coalition, and the CEDA's biggest partner in the previous elections, the Radicals, had all but disintegrated. Gil Robles worked to construct a broad, counter-revolutionary alliance. The highly personal – not to say corrupt – nature of Spanish politics at local level made a variety of deals possible. Monarchists, Carlists, some Radicals, the conservative Catalan Lliga, Agrarians, even a few Liberal Democrats featured as part of the alliance in one electoral district or another, all of them attracted by the CEDA's numerical strength.

Gil Robles knew that the stakes were high, and threw money, energy and modern advertising techniques into the campaign. Unprecedented numbers of leaflets and pamphlets were distributed. A portrait of Gil Robles himself that took up three whole storeys dominated the central Puerta del Sol in Madrid. Every effort was made to cajole, persuade or frighten voters into the ranks of the counter-revolution. The youth wing of the CEDA (the JAP) was even less restrained than Gil Robles himself in calling for full powers for their leader, or *jefe*. Opponents

feared that a CEDA triumph would lead to a fascist takeover of the Republic.

The vigorous campaign was successful, in that the vote for the right-wing coalition was increased by more than 750,000 votes over the 1933 result. But it did not produce the desired majority. On the contrary, an opposing electoral alliance, the Popular Front, did even better. The grand strategy to reclaim the Republic for property, order, family and religion had failed. Almost immediately, some of the generals began to plan a military coup.

The Popular Front was an anti-fascist pact. Indalecio Prieto, in exile or in hiding after the failure of the October 1934 revolution, encouraged the Socialist party during 1935 to resume its previous, democratic strategy, since the attempt to seize power by revolution had failed. He argued that the Socialists could not win an election by themselves, and that they must be part of a wider coalition to stop the right. In spite of resistance from Largo Caballero and the Socialist youth movement (FJS), who wanted a Bolshevik rather than a parliamentary strategy, his arguments won the day inside the PSOE. Azaña persuaded various Republican groups to join forces with the Socialists. The Communists also joined, in accordance with the Communist International's new policy of making common cause with any political formation that opposed fascism. By the end of 1935, when Alcalá-Zamora dissolved parliament and called new elections, the Popular Front electoral alliance was ready.

Its programme was a repeat of 1931. The Republicans would not allow the inclusion of long-term Socialist aims, such as the nationalisation of land or industry. So agreement was reached on a minimal programme of amnesty for the prisoners of

October 1934, civil rights and the reforms of the first *bienio*. From the point of view of those on the left of the Socialist party, not to mention the openly revolutionary movements beyond them, the content of the Popular Front agreement signed on 15 January 1936 was disappointingly slight. Nonetheless, it proved the basis of an electoral victory. A small majority of perhaps as few as 200,000 votes translated into a great cascade of seats in parliament. In the new Cortes, there were 280 Popular Front deputies, to 190 of all other parties combined. The CEDA now had 87 seats instead of its previous 115. The Republic was once more in the hands of its creators.

The Popular Front's commitment to reinstate the social legislation of 1931–33 filled Spanish conservatives with dread. The Agrarian Reform Law, devolution, legal restraints on employers, and the secularising of marriage and education were not acceptable to them. The prospect of further land redistribution conjured up visions of social revolution. Nor could they tolerate once more being forbidden by the state to send their children to Catholic schools. Gil Robles consulted army chiefs to see if they were willing to use force immediately to prevent the assumption of power by the Popular Front, and to install him as Prime Minister. They were not, though that did not mean that they accepted the legitimacy of a Popular Front government. On 19 February, Manuel Azaña became Prime Minister.

In some respects, however, February 1936 was not a rerun of the early Republic. The Socialist party, in which Largo Caballero was now the dominant figure, was determined not to repeat what it saw as the mistake of its alliance with the Republicans. The Popular Front electoral coalition did not translate into a coalition government. Instead, the Republicans, with no mass base in the country, were left to govern.

Even worse was to follow when Indalecio Prieto foolishly attacked President Alcalá-Zamora in parliament in April, arguing that his decision twice to dissolve the Cortes and call new elections was an abuse of power. Alcalá-Zamora, distrusted by both left and right, was removed from office. Azaña succeeded him. But when, in May, President Azaña asked Prieto to form a government, the Socialist party refused to back Prieto. Just when the Republic needed a strong coalition government, with mass support, it got instead a weak cabinet of little-known Republicans, with one of their number, Santiago Casares Quiroga, as Prime Minister. This was a poor response to the popular vote of February.

Meanwhile, a different kind of politics was taking over, on the land, on the streets and in the homes of military plotters. For tens of thousands of agricultural labourers in southern and western Spain, land ownership remained the central issue. This was as true of the landworkers enrolled in the Socialist agrarian union, the FNTT, as it was of their Anarchist counterparts in the CNT. They had looked to the Republic for land and social justice in 1931. Now, after the conservative reaction of the 'black' years of 1934 and 1935, with the dismantling of wage arbitration committees, falling wages and rising unemployment, they were desperate.

Peasants temporarily occupied land in several parts of the country in the spring of 1936, and in Badajoz they simply seized land as their own. Their illegal action was accepted as a *fait accompli* by a well-intentioned government determined to ease the plight of the rural poor. As far as the estate-owners were concerned, however, this was tantamount to an abdication of governmental responsibility. Indeed, it was the revolution already in progress. At the same time, reconstituted wage arbitration committees that made decisions in favour of agricultural workers inevitably alienated employers. Labour relations on the great estates were those of class war.

Slippage away from respect for the law, and towards direct action, was also evident in Spain's cities, including Madrid. After the CEDA's failure in the February elections, the Spanish fascist party, the Falange, grew substantially, and absorbed members of the CEDA's youth section. The Falange had never pretended that it was a parliamentary movement, and in 1936 it turned increasingly to violence. At the other end of the political spectrum, the small Spanish Communist party (PCE) also benefited from disillusion with the political process. In April, the youth sections of the Socialists and the Communists merged, forming the United Young Socialists (JSU), which was in fact Communist dominated. They and the Falangists were involved in armed confrontations and assassination attempts.

Violence on the streets laid the government open to the charge of not being in control of public order. There were over 250 violent deaths between February and July, and it was tit-for-tat killings that triggered the start of civil war on 17 July. Meanwhile, the impression of lawlessness was increased in May by a great wave of strikes, notably among construction workers in Madrid, but spreading far beyond them. Anarchist strikers disregarded appeals to return to work, and demanded a new social order. Militants were outflanking politicians on the left as well as on the right, and militia groups were forming on both sides. On 16 June, Gil Robles denounced the government for widespread disorder, while himself undermining it by his complicity in army plots. He, like other conservative politicians, really abandoned the Republic long before the attempted coup in July.

The victory of the Popular Front shifted the initiative in conservative Spain away from the politicians to the generals. Azaña recognised this, and as a precaution his government reassigned General Goded to the Balearic Islands, and sent General Mola to distant Navarre, and General Franco to the even more distant Canary Islands, out of harm's way. Nevertheless, as early as March, discussions began about a military rising. General Sanjurjo was the obvious leader, but was still in exile in Portugal.

The central figure in the planning stage was General Mola. Others involved included Generals Fanjul, Villegas, Varela, Orgaz and Saliquet, and Sanjurjo's representative Colonel Valentín Galarza. Franco was in

touch with developing plans, but remained non-committal until a later date. Behind the leading generals stood a large number of officers in the Spanish Military Union (UME), a conservative association founded in 1933, who were eager for action. Civilian politicians who were aware that plots were being hatched, and supported them, included Gil Robles, the monarchist leader José Calvo Sotelo, the Carlist leader Fal Conde and the head of the Falange, José Antonio Primo de Rivera. In comparison with this array, the only conservative political groups still committed to the Republic were the small number of moderate Republicans round Alcalá-Zamora and Miguel Maura, and the Basque Nationalists, who disliked authoritarian centralism even more than they disliked the Popular Front's anti-clericalism.

By the end of June, the military coup was prepared, and commanding generals had been assigned to each of the eight military districts of Spain. The success of any coup, however, was far from certain. Republican officers formed a loyal alternative to the UME, called the Republican Anti-Fascist Military Union (UMRA). Several generals were loyal to the Republic. The Republican government, fearful of a coup, had amassed loyal armed police units in the capital. Masses of rural and urban workers still looked to the Republic for a better life. The government, however, in spite of numerous warnings of impending danger, made no direct move to foil the reported plot.

Many Spaniards began their summer holidays in early July, as usual. But on 12 July, Lieutenant José Castillo of the Assault Guards (a militarised police force founded as an urban equivalent of the Civil Guards), who was himself a member of the UMRA, was shot dead by a group of Falangists. In reprisal, Assault Guards set out to kill a conservative politician. They could not find their first two targets, one of whom was Gil Robles, and so killed the third, the monarchist leader José Calvo Sotelo, who had been Finance Minister in the late 1920s. The manner of his death was particularly shocking. He was taken from his house in Madrid by uniformed Assault Guards in a police car. They carried authorisation for his arrest. They drove him away, shot him and left his body in the Madrid public morgue, where it was identified on the morning of 13 July. A major political leader had been killed while in the custody of law enforcement officers. It was not surprising that Spanish conservatives concluded that the government had lost control, since it was unable even to stop its own officers dealing out a summary death penalty as though the law and the courts did not exist.

Calvo Sotelo's murder provoked the plotters to fix a definite date for the rising that was anyway planned for some time in July. General Franco had by now committed himself to the enterprise. On 11 July, Luís Bolín, a monarchist journalist, chartered a Dragon Rapide aeroplane in Croydon. On the 14th, it was in Las Palmas, ready to fly Franco to Morocco, where he was to assume command. The rising began in Spanish Morocco on Friday 17 July, a day earlier than planned, because of fears that the plot would be discovered. It was followed on the Spanish mainland by numerous military risings over the next two days. Although the coup was successful in Morocco, Pamplona, Burgos, Valladolid, Cádiz, Córdoba, Jerez and Seville, it failed in Madrid, Barcelona, Oviedo, Bilbao, Badajoz and Málaga. Spain was divided militarily and geographically, as well as politically. The Spanish Civil War had begun.

Spain divides

The initial division of forces and resources was unsatisfactory to both Republicans and rebels. The rebels lost their leader, General Sanjurjo, in a plane crash as he set off from Portugal on 20 July 1936 to take command in Burgos. They held Spanish Morocco, where Franco had reached Tetuán on the 19th, after the rising had already succeeded. Franco therefore had the Army of Africa at his command, and a small detachment of the air force, which had attempted resistance but been overwhelmed. But he faced the problem of how to get his formidable forces to the mainland, since the crews on board Spanish ships in the Mediterranean disobeyed their rebel naval officers, executed them and remained loyal to the Republic. Cadiz, held by the rebel generals Varela and López Pinto, could not be reached. Beyond it, Queipo de Llano took Seville, including the airport. This permitted a group of the Foreign Legion to fly there from Morocco in a Fokker, and take part in the merciless assault on the working-class district of Triana. But the rest of the forces in north Africa were stuck.

The rising also triumphed in the agrarian conservative heartlands of Old Castile, Navarre and the far north-west, including the naval base of El Ferrol. But it failed along most of the north coast, including Bilbao with its all-important iron and steel works, and across a great swathe of central, eastern and north-eastern Spain, including Madrid, and the great industrial city of Barcelona. Not only was north Africa cut off from southern Spain by Republican ships, but western Andalusia was cut off from rebel territory in the north. It was impossible for anyone to exercise overall command. Moreover, army officers were not the undisputed leaders everywhere of the rebellion. In Navarre, General Mola was well aware of the strength of the Carlist militias. Elsewhere, Falangist militias or monarchist activists operated independently, and in many towns where there was no military garrison, they led the rising. Meanwhile the Falange leader, José Antonio Primo de Rivera, was in a Republican prison far away in Alicante.

On the government side, it was depressing enough that within just a few days about a third of the country was in the hands of its enemies. But the military rebellion sparked a furious popular reaction that stripped the government, and the Republican state, of authority. Everywhere trade unionists and left-wing parties demanded that arms be distributed to them. Prime Minister Casares Quiroga resisted these demands on 18 July, then resigned. President Azaña appointed Diego Martínez Barrio in his place, who tried futilely to win over General Mola, then also resigned early on the 19th.

The new Prime Minister was José Giral, who took the inevitable step of arming the Madrid proletariat by supplying the Socialist and Anarchist trade unions with army rifles. When the Madrid garrisons were ordered to hand over the bolts that the rifles needed, they refused. General Fanjul, leader of the rebellion in Madrid, was trapped in the Montaña barracks by crowds of hostile workers, some of them now armed. Giral's decision to arm left-wing organisations was also implemented elsewhere. Power seeped away from the government to the streets, and from the institutions of the state to the revolutionary masses.

On 20 July the Montaña barracks were attacked by the crowds, aided by a few aircraft, some artillery, and loyal Assault Guards and Civil Guards. Fanjul's forces, numbering about 2,000, with about 150 additional right-wing sympathisers, replied with machine-guns. But at noon the assault

Soldiers involved in the armed rising in Barcelona in July 1936 collect ammunition. But in Barcelona, as in Madrid, the rising failed because arms were also distributed to workers, who joined forces with loyal Assault Guards and prevented the soldiers garrisoned in Spain's two most important cities from gaining control of them. (Roger-Viollet)

succeeded, and crowds surged into the courtyard of the barracks, fighting hand to hand with its defenders. Several hundred people died. Fanjul was imprisoned, and in the following month court-martialled and shot. The other Madrid garrisons were either persuaded into loyalty or overwhelmed.

Events in Barcelona were similar, except that the rebel plan there was for the troops of the various garrisons, about 5,000 men in all, to converge on the Plaza de Catalunya in the centre, and then take the city. The President of the autonomous government of Catalonia, Luis Companys, had refused to distribute arms to the masses, just as Casares Quiroga and Martínez Barrio had done. But he could not prevent some Guards doing so independently. Approximately 5,000 loyal Assault and Civil Guards, some police and crowds of Anarchists, a few of them now armed, fought bravely with the columns of infantrymen making their way to the Plaza de Catalunya. They prevented the planned meeting there, and took control of the city, completing it with an attack on the Atarazanas barracks on the night of 20–21 July. At least 500 people died in the confrontation in Barcelona. General Goded was taken prisoner, and in August was tried for military rebellion and shot. Local air bases remained loyal.

In several other places, the outcome of the rising was in doubt in the first days. In Oviedo, centre of the October 1934 revolution, the local military commander, Colonel Antonio Aranda, assured miners' leaders that the city was safe in his hands. After they set off by train to help defend Madrid on 19 July, he claimed the city for the rebels. His actions produced the extraordinary phenomenon of a city thoroughly identified with revolutionary fervour falling without a fight into the camp of counter-revolution. But Oviedo was isolated in hostile Republican territory.

At the other end of the country, Granada was similarly isolated, a rebel city in the middle of an anti-rebel area, after the military commander, General Muñoz, was imprisoned by rebel officers, and the working-class quarter violently subdued. In many cities, the issue was decided by the personal decision for or against the rising made by the commanding officer, as was the case in Badajoz, with General Luis Castelló (for the government), and Córdoba, with Colonel Ciriaco Cascajo (for the rebels). Sometimes, however, the commanding officer discovered that no one was following him. General José Bosch was prevented by his own troops from taking Minorca for the rebels, even though in Majorca and Ibiza they had triumphed.

Whether the rebels had to fight to gain control, or triumphed easily, their success was followed by the immediate, violent repression of those identified with the Popular Front. Members of the left-wing parties, trade unionists and freemasons were killed by rebel soldiers, Civil Guards, Carlists and Falangists, acting either on direct orders from the military commanding officer, or on their own initiative. Sometimes there was a summary trial, often not. Even where the rebels were obviously in complete control locally, such as in Navarre, rightist gangs summarily arrested political opponents, drove them out of the town or village, and shot them by the roadside. This terror was to intimidate, control and punish.

By 20 July it was obvious that, where the rising failed, the government nonetheless was not the victor. Anarchists, Socialists and Communists ruled the streets, setting up anti-fascist, revolutionary committees. As Luis Companys, President of the Catalan regional government, acknowledged to Anarchist leaders in Barcelona, 'Today, you are the masters of the city.' Except in the Republican Basque provinces of Vizcaya and Guipúzcoa, where the moderate Basque Nationalist party (PNV) dominated, revolutionary terror was directed against propertied elites, conservative politicians and the church. Except in the Basque country, Catholicism went underground in Republican Spain, as churches burned and religious images were destroyed.

The violence on both sides was sickening, sharpened by the class hatreds and cultural conflicts that had marked Spanish history for decades. The army officers who took up arms against the Republic in July 1936 bore the immediate responsibility for unleashing the whirlwind of violence. They argued, however, that the violence began not in July 1936, but in the revolution of October 1934, and that the Popular Front was the illegitimate continuation of the forces which made that revolution. This controversial claim was used in July 1936, and continuously thereafter, even when the war was over, to justify repression, reprisals and summary justice.

After the patchy fortunes of the coup, and after the first days of fighting, about 13 million Spaniards found themselves still in Republican Spain, which also contained almost all major industry and the financial reserves of the Bank of Spain. About 11 million were in territory taken by the rebels, now arrogating to themselves the title of 'nationals', or Nationalists. This territory at least had the advantage of including some of Spain's most productive wheat-growing areas.

The Spanish army on the mainland and in the Balearic and Canary Islands numbered something over 60,000 men at the time of the coup. It was organised into eight territorial divisions on the mainland, one in the Canary Islands and another in the Balearic Islands. Each of the mainland divisions had two infantry brigades, one artillery brigade and support units. Just over half were in Republican territory, the rest in Nationalist. In addition, the Army of Africa in rebel-held Morocco numbered about 25,000. It comprised five infantry battalions, six Foreign Legion *banderas* or battalions, 30 *tabores* or half-battalions of indigenous Moroccan Regulars, plus artillery, cavalry and engineers.

The Foreign Legion was the creation of José Millán Astray, a crazed militarist, and was renowned for its ruthless daring. It was a last resort for desperate men. Later in the war, Millán Astray caused a commotion when he shouted 'Death to intelligence' and the Legion's blood-curdling slogan 'Long live death' at Spain's most revered philosopher,

Miguel Unamuno, in Salamanca University. It was one of the most bizarre cultural confrontations of the war.

There were also about 80,000 men serving in the militarised law enforcement organisations – approximately 34,000 Civil Guards, over 31,000 Assault Guards and nearly 15,000 carabineers. The majority remained with the Republic – about 20,000 Civil Guards, 22,000 Assault Guards and 9,000 carabineers. On paper, therefore, the two sides seemed to have roughly equal numerical strength, with the Republic's advantage in the militarised security forces roughly balancing the Nationalists' control of the Army of Africa. Rifles, bayonets and artillery pieces were split between the two sides, although many of the rifles were pre-1914 issue, and ammunition was often in short supply.

Both sides needed to recruit and train soldiers swiftly, and both began enlisting men as soon as possible. Both sides set up very abbreviated officers' training courses, and the Nationalists used non-commissioned as well as commissioned officers. On both sides, men complained about lack of training, lack of ammunition, and old, poorly functioning equipment. But the impression of balance is misleading. Many of the conscripts on Republican territory simply left their posts in the confusion and melted away, while only a minority of officers were considered reliable. Moreover, the forces in north Africa were trained, disciplined and experienced, in stark contrast to the situation of many soldiers in mainland garrisons.

The Spanish air force was small. In late July 1936, the government had about 200 planes and the Nationalists about 100 – in both cases a mixture of reconnaissance planes (mainly Breguet XIX), fighters (mainly Nieuports) and bombers (a mixture of Fokker VIIs, De Havilland Dragons and Douglas DC2s). The government could count on a battleship, three cruisers, 20 destroyers and 12 submarines, but the commanding officers of many of these had been killed by mutinous crews, who were loyal but lacked expertise. The Nationalists fared less well, with one

A Spanish government plane in action in September 1936, bombing a
rebel position. The small Spanish Air Force remained loyal to the
Republic. German and Italian planes were sent to Franco in Spanish
Morocco within days of the military rising. By early November Soviet
planes were in action to bolster the Republic. (Topham Picturepoint)

battleship, two cruisers, one destroyer and two submarines. Moreover, the government had over two-thirds of the merchant shipping.

Where new production was concerned, the Republic controlled the major arms factories, and the Nationalists the major naval dockyard at El Ferrol. All in all, considering territory, population, financial resources, industry, agriculture and armaments, the government looked better supplied for a long struggle, but had to rebuild its army, and translate the enthusiasm of the popular militias based on the left-wing parties and trade unions into military effectiveness. The rebels lacked industrial strength, but had greater military control of their (divided) territory. In these circumstances, in which neither side was assured of victory and both urgently needed arms, it was inevitable that both would look beyond Spain for foreign assistance. Within days of its outbreak, the Spanish Civil War would become an international problem.

War, revolution and international involvement

Madrid and Barcelona

Madrid and Barcelona were the two great Republican triumphs in July 1936. Each city had over one million inhabitants, dwarfing other cities in Spain. Valencia, the next largest, was less than one-third that size, followed by Seville with a population of about 250,000. Holding on to Madrid and Barcelona was vital for the Republic, and winning them was a necessary aim of the Nationalists.

In the short term, nothing could be done about Barcelona, which was surrounded by Republican territory, with secure land access to the French frontier, and protected by sea by ships under Republican control. Indeed,

almost 20,000 Anarchists, left-Catalans, Socialists, Communists and anti-Stalinist Communists in the POUM, with a small number of regular soldiers, set off from Barcelona to take the war and the revolution west into Aragón. They got within sight of Saragossa before the front settled in a wiggling, north–south line that crossed the River Ebro south-east of the city. Notwithstanding the bravery of militia

Volunteers leaving Madrid on 29 July 1936 surrounded by cheering crowds. Once the attempted rising in Madrid had been defeated, volunteers rushed to the Guadarrama hills to prevent rebel forces commanded by General Mola from taking the city from the north. In bitter fighting they succeeded. (Topham Picturepoint)

'They shall not pass.' Republican Civil War poster illustrating the
defence of Madrid by young men and women volunteers. The
great Communist orator, Dolores Ibárruri (*La Pasionaria*) made
'They shall not pass' the rallying slogan of Republican Madrid, as
rebel forces attempted to take it, first from the north, then
from the south-west. (Author's collection)

leaders like Durruti, and the maverick direct hit from the air on the shrine of the Virgin of the Pillar in the Saragossa basilica – the bomb, some thought miraculously, did not explode – the motley Republican forces advanced no further for another 18 months.

Madrid was a very different matter from Barcelona. Right in the centre of Spain, where Philip II had decided back in the 16th century the capital should be, it was protected by Republican territory all the way south to the Mediterranean. But to the north-east, north, north-west and west, only a narrow arc of land lay between it and Nationalist Spain. Madrid looked vulnerable. On 19 and 20 July young men, and some young women too, had grabbed rifles and converged on the rebel garrisons in Madrid, which they took with the aid of loyal armed Assault Guards. Once this heroic task was accomplished, they commandeered lorries

Republican militia women in the Spanish Civil War. Women as well as men seized rifles and went to the front to defend the Republic in the first phase of the war. Many also began to wear practical, unisex dungarees - the mono. Francoists considered this military role for women a perversion. (AKG, Berlin. and Aisa)

Republican militiamen surrendering to rebel forces at the Somosierra pass, in one of the battles in the Guadarrama hills to the north of Madrid. Although General Mola's forces gained control of this pass, they were not able to advance any further. (Aisa)

and rushed out of the city to defend the northern approaches from rebel advances. These improvised militias, wearing blue workers' overalls and dungarees instead of military uniform, headed for the Guadarrama hills to the north-west and north, and surged north-east to the towns of Alcalá and Guadalajara, both of which they took from rebel garrisons.

Meanwhile, General Mola sent Colonel García Escámez, some troops and about 1,000 Nationalist militia composed of armed Carlists, called *requetés*, and Falangists, south from Navarre towards Guadalajara. But they were unable to reach it – the first of many efforts to reach Madrid had failed. García Escámez then circled round east to the Somosierra pass, almost due north of Madrid, to hold it for the Nationalists on 25 July. At the same time, other Nationalist forces headed down from Valladolid to the Alto del Léon pass between Avilá and Segovia, which

they took on the 22nd. Lack of ammunition, however, as well as determined Republican resistance, prevented these various columns under Mola's ultimate command from getting any closer to Madrid. Republicans continued to hold the major pass between Somosierra and Alto del Léon, at Navacerrada, right to the end of the war. For a while the front stabilised. At some points it was only 40 miles (64 km) north-west of the capital.

. This early fighting was brave and brutal on both sides, setting a pattern that would continue in the long struggle for territorial domination. On both sides, too, the militias were vitally important. The Communists were soonest and best organised among the Republicans, with militia groups in Madrid swiftly being incorporated into the new Communist Fifth Regiment, under leaders like Juan Modesto and Enrique Lister. But the existence of separate Anarchist, Socialist and Communist columns represented an enormous problem as well as a resource for the government. They were determined to retain their own political identity and autonomy, even at the front. The most revolutionary militias, the Anarchists and the POUM, would not obey orders they

General José Sanjurjo, 1932. On 10 August 1932 the monarchist General Sanjurjo attempted a coup against the Second Republic in Seville. It failed. Sanjurjo was imprisoned, then later released and went into exile in Portugal. From there he directed the conspiracy which resulted in the rising of July 1936, but he was killed in a plane crash as he set off to lead it. (Topham Picturepoint)

Republican areas, were overwhelmed. Militias from Valencia then advanced as far north as Teruel, the south-east extreme of rebel territory, though they failed to take it. The Nationalists also made some gains. In particular, General Queipo de Llano extended his control across the south-west corner of the country, linking the towns already in rebel hands by conquering the surrounding countryside. Two weeks after the initial risings, the Republic was stronger in the east and north, the Nationalists in the south-west, but the overall balance of forces had not changed dramatically.

International involvement

Both sides attempted to alter the balance by drawing in external resources. On his very first, turbulent day in office on 19 July, Prime Minister Giral telegrammed the new French Prime Minister, Léon Blum, a Socialist, to ask for arms and aeroplanes. The Spanish ambassador in Paris followed up the initial request with a precise list of what was wanted – bombers, machine-guns, howitzers and rifles, all with their appropriate ammunition – before he, a Nationalist, resigned.

Blum and his Foreign and War Ministers (both Radicals) agreed to the Spanish government's request, but then had to deal with countervailing influences from the British government and right-wing opinion in France, and obstruction from Nationalist Spanish embassy officials in Paris. The result was a mixture of retreat and subterfuge, in which the coalition French government declared on 25 July that it would not, after all, send arms to Spain, but its Air Minister, Pierre Cot, secretly permitted a consignment

disagreed with. Militias based on the various trade unions and left-wing parties were instinctively suspicious of army leaders, and often with good reason: for instance, General Luis Castelló, appointed Minister of War on 19 July, fled to France early in August.

Apart from the action around Madrid, and in Aragón, local changes in military control occurred in several other places in late July. Rebel garrisons in San Sebastián and Valencia, which were enclaves in

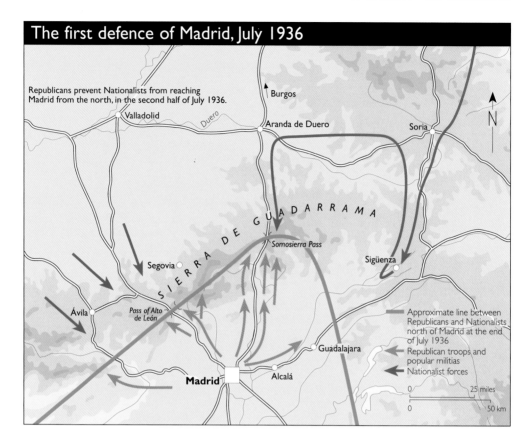

The first defence of Madrid, July 1936

Republicans prevent Nationalists from reaching
Madrid from the north, in the second half of July 1936.

Burgos

Valladolid

Duero

Aranda de Duero

Soria

N

SIERRA DE GUADARRAMA

Somosierra Pass

Segovia

Sigüenza

Ávila

Pass of Alto
de León

Guadalajara

Madrid

Alcalá

Approximate line between
Republicans and Nationalists
north of Madrid at the end
of July 1936

Republican troops and
popular militias

Nationalist forces

0   25 miles

0   50 km

of aircraft to be dispatched. At the end of
July, about 70 aircraft were sent across the
border to Barcelona, including Potez 54
bombers and Dewoitine 371 fighters.

The Popular Front government in France
was divided, and subjected to two quite
different pressures. One was the desire to
bolster another government that had come
into office as the result of a Popular Front
electoral victory, against a right-wing coup
that would create a pro-fascist Spain. But the
other was a fear of alienating France's most
important diplomatic partner, Britain, whose
Conservative government in 1936, with
Stanley Baldwin as Prime Minister and
Anthony Eden as Foreign Secretary, was
concerned above all to limit the conflict to
Spain and prevent escalation.

Moreover, the accounts of revolution,
expropriations and anti-clerical atrocities in
Republican Spain frightened conservatives
everywhere. Selling arms to a democratically
elected government threatened by a military

coup was one thing. Aiding an atheistic social
revolution that killed priests and landlords was
quite another. Internal and external pressures
forced Blum to ban all exports of war material
to Spain, even by private companies, from
9 August. Procuring arms was going to be a
major, and crippling, problem for the Republic.

It was as obvious to Mola and to Franco as
it was to Prime Minister Giral that external
supplies could make a decisive difference. On
19 July Franco sent Luís Bolín on the next
stage of his extraordinary trip in the Dragon
Rapide that had already flown from Croydon
to the Canary Islands and on to Morocco.
The next destination was Rome, where on
the 22nd Bolín saw Foreign Minister Ciano to
ask for 12 bombers and three fighter-planes.
Mussolini hesitated, but two factors swayed
him. Leading Spanish monarchists, to whom
he had promised support back in 1934, were
sent to Rome by Mola to support Franco's
request. And news of the French
government's decision not to provide arms to

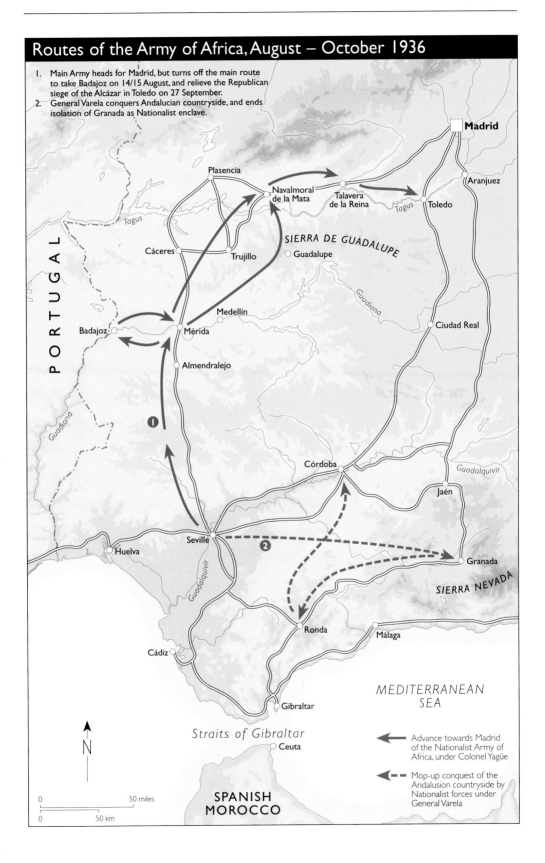

Routes of the Army of Africa, August – October 1936

1. Main Army heads for Madrid, but turns off the main route to take Badajoz on 14/15 August, and relieve the Republican siege of the Alcázar in Toledo on 27 September.
2. General Varela conquers Andalucian countryside, and ends isolation of Granada as Nationalist enclave.

Madrid

Aranjuez

Plasencia

Navalmoral de la Mata

Talavera de la Reina

Tagus

Toledo

PORTUGAL

Cáceres

Trujillo

SIERRA DE GUADALUPE

Guadalupe

Guadiana

Ciudad Real

Medellín

Badajoz

Mérida

Almendralejo

Guadiana

Córdoba

Guadalquivir

Jaén

Seville

Huelva

Guadalquivir

Granada

SIERRA NEVADA

Ronda

Málaga

Cádiz

Gibraltar

MEDITERRANEAN SEA

N

Straits of Gibraltar

Ceuta

SPANISH MOROCCO

0   50 miles

0   50 km

← Advance towards Madrid of the Nationalist Army of Africa, under Colonel Yagüe

◄--- Mop-up conquest of the Andalusion countryside by Nationalist forces under General Varela

the Republic reassured him that he would not risk direct confrontation with France over Spain. He promised to send 12 Savoia 81 bombers to Franco in Morocco.

Both Franco and Mola sent urgent requests for arms to Germany, through German Foreign Office officials. Neither prospered because the Foreign Minister, Neurath, and his senior staff saw no advantage to Germany, and many disadvantages, in such involvement in Spain. But a different approach from Franco, through the Nazi party, direct to Hitler, was successful. On 23 July Adolph Langenheim and Johannes Bernhardt, Nazis based in north Africa, set off with a Spanish air force officer to convey Franco's personal request to Hitler. They met him on the 25th, after a performance of *Siegfried* at Bayreuth. Without even consulting the Foreign Minister, Hitler agreed to provide planes. A German company, ROWAK, was set up to handle supplies, both from the government and from German companies, and a Spanish company, HISMA, was established to handle distribution and payments, in money or raw materials, especially ores. Six Heinkels, 51 fighter-planes and 20 Junkers 52s which could be used for transport or as bombers, were dispatched to Morocco. On 29 July the first consignments reached Morocco, as did nine of Mussolini's Savoia 81 bombers, the other three having either crashed or been forced to land short of their target. The Junkers began ferrying Franco's forces to Seville, the first major airlift of its kind in military history, while bombers provided air cover for merchant ships carrying men and equipment across the Mediterranean.

Army of Africa

The arrival of the Army of Africa in Andalusia created the first radical change in the balance of forces in Spain. It also gave Franco the opportunity to establish himself as the leading military figure among the Nationalists, a project that was greatly enhanced by his privileged status as the unique recipient of German aid. Franco flew to Seville on 6 August

to oversee operations, while Yagüe was the field commander of about 8,000 men.

The obvious strategy was to head north towards Madrid. There were two possible routes. One, somewhat shorter, swung north-east through Córdoba and approached Madrid via Aranjuez. Taking this route, however, would have meant leaving Republican territory to the west, which separated the two parts of Nationalist Spain and also gave the Republic a border in southern Extremadura with Portugal. The more westerly route lay through Mérida and Trujillo and thence along the Tagus valley, finally approaching Madrid via Talavera de la Reina. Franco opted for this second alternative.

Each *bandera* of the Legion – a battalion of 600 men – was accompanied by a *tabor* of the indigenous Moroccan Regulars – a half battalion of 225 men – together with artillery, under a commanding officer. They were transported in lorries, with air cover from eight Savoias 81 and nine Junkers 52s, flown by their Italian and German pilots. The army travelled at remarkable speed, and reached Mérida, nearly 200 miles (320 km) north of Seville, in under a week on 10 August. Its methods were direct. Air and artillery fire prepared the assault on towns along the way. Sometimes that was enough to enable the troops to walk in. Sometimes they had to fight their way in, usually against local militias, with Mérida itself much the most difficult battle of this first week. Everywhere they took few prisoners, killing those who had fought against them and not managed to escape, and also killing local political and trade union leaders. As news of their advance and their methods spread, a terrified population tried to flee out of their path, together with retreating militias.

The Legion and the Moroccan soldiers immediately became a byword for cruelty. Part of the reason for this lay in the ethos and earlier experience of both of these forces, forged in harsh colonial wars in north Africa. They behaved in Spain like a particularly ruthless, lawless, army in dangerous territory. Another part of the reason was their relatively small number. They did not have the resources to leave large detachments behind to enforce law and order. Terror was easier. Finally, they acted to revenge the social revolution provoked by the July risings, and the atrocities perpetrated against clergy and property-owners.

In Almendralejo, for example, south of Mérida, the revolutionary committee imprisoned local right-wingers, and then, treating them as hostages as the rebel forces advanced, killed some of them by setting fire to them and pelting them with hand grenades. Far greater numbers were to die in the reprisals. As far as Yagüe's army was concerned, the local population was a revolutionary rabble with blood on its hands. Closed churches were reopened. Priests and landlords who had survived the days of proletarian power came out of hiding. Order of a kind was imposed, based on fear and repression. After the fall of Mérida, Yagüe's men were joined by a column from Cáceres, in the first meeting of forces from the two blocks of rebel territory.

The capture of Badajoz, on the Portuguese frontier, stands out even in the orgy of violence as exceptionally bloody. Following Franco's directives, Yagüe turned west to take it, rather than leave a fortified town in Republican hands at his rear. Its city walls, the River Guadiana to its east, and the presence of about 6,000 militiamen and armed forces, with artillery and planes, made Badajoz a difficult target. On 14 August Legionaries launched a suicidally brave advance against defence artillery at one of the city gates, Trinidad, with exceptionally heavy losses. At the second try, survivors managed to fight through, and met other Legionaries who had forced an entry by other gates, inside the city. They pursued their opponents, killing many in hand-to-hand combat, and rounding up others, including some women, into the bullring.

Almost 2,000 people were shot, on Yagüe's orders, on 14 and 15 August, the eve and feast day of the Assumption of the Virgin Mary, a major festival in the calendar of the Catholic Church. This horrifying slaughter, which continued over the next few days,

immediately became known as the massacre of Badajoz. No one and nowhere was safe. Men who retreated into the cathedral were killed there, and others who fled across the border into Portugal were executed when the Portuguese authorities handed them over. The Nationalist forces drew no distinctions between battle, and policy after the battle was won. Reprisals were used as part of a rough strategy to leave no effective enemies in the rear, to intimidate the population and to wipe out the alternative Spain represented by Badajoz's defenders.

The Nationalists now controlled west Spain from La Corunna in the north to Cádiz in the south, including the whole of the frontier with Portugal. On 26 August Franco moved his centre of operations north to Cáceres. Meanwhile, in southern Andalusia, Colonel Varela mopped up the countryside between the rebel strongholds of Seville, Córdoba and Granada.

The main Army of Africa resumed its advance through Extremadura towards Navalmoral de la Mata, north of the River Tagus. Republican aeroplanes and General Riquelme's soldiers and militias operating from the central zone attacked them from the east, successfully at Medellín, unsuccessfully at Guadalupe and then Navalmoral itself. Securing Guadalupe, a small mountain town dominated by a historic monastery and shrine to the Virgin Mary, was a symbolic triumph for Franco's forces.

This part of Extremadura was classic conquistador country, from where the conquistadores had taken the devotion to the Virgin of Guadalupe to America. Trujillo, between Mérida and Navalmoral, was Francisco Pizarro's birthplace. Hernán Cortés's hometown of Medellín would only fall to the Nationalists two years later, in July 1938. Securing these territories meant forging a link between the Spanish, Catholic conquest of South America, and Franco's Catholic reconquest of Spain itself. It was a link that the Franco regime would always emphasise, no more troubled at the cruelty and bloodshed of the modern crusade than at that of Ferdinand and Isabella over

The Spanish Foreign Legion in Morocco, July 1936, waiting to board a German transport plane that would fly them to Seville. From there, they advanced rapidly through southern Spain towards Madrid. Without Hitler's intervention, Franco's forces in Morocco, including the Army of Africa, indigenous troops, and the Foreign Legion, would have been stranded. (Topham Picturepoint)

1,197 officers, men and Civil Guards, more than 100 right-wing civilian activists, mainly of the Falange, and over 500 women and children, including some nuns. There were also about 100 left-wing hostages. They lived on corn and horsemeat. On 21 September they were still holding out, but with very few supplies left, in spite of repeated bombardments, artillery and arson attacks, which had destroyed large sections of the fortress. Moscardó's resilience had become a Nationalist symbol, intensified by his famous refusal to surrender even when Republicans put his son Luís on the telephone on 23 July to explain that, if his father held out, he, Luís, would be killed. Colonel Moscardó refused. Luís was executed a month later.

It was typical of Franco that he rated the relief of the Toledo fortress as more urgent than the advance on Madrid. His troops were too close to it for him to be able to ignore Moscardó's situation, with its symbolic potency. The Nationalists fought their way into the city, and wreaked vengeance on its defenders and citizens not only for their attacks on the Alcázar, but also for murdering priests and right-wingers. One-half of the clergy of the archdiocese of Toledo had been killed in the early stages of the war. Toledo was the historic centre of Spanish Catholicism, and the archbishopric of Toledo was the most senior church office in the country. Victory here, as elsewhere, was not just military conquest but also counter-revolution. Nonetheless, it was a costly strategy: Madrid was better defended when Franco's army eventually reached its outskirts at the end of October than it had been a month earlier.

400 years earlier. Nor would the regime's apologists be embarrassed that this Christian crusade owed much of its success to Islamic Regulars from Morocco and pagan Nazis.

Naval moral was firmly under rebel control by 23 August 1936, and became a military and air base. From there, the major obstacle on the way to Madrid was Talavera de la Reina, which the Nationalists reached on 2 September. Even though the town was defended by several thousand militiamen and artillery, it fell within a day. Madrid was now less than 70 miles (110 km) away. The rebels pressed on, encountering repeated, but ultimately ineffective, Republican attacks, and taking Maqueda on the 21st. Perhaps if they had headed straight for Madrid, as planned, they might have broken through its defences. But at this point Franco, to Yagüe's dismay, instead ordered his forces to march 25 miles (40 km) south-west to Toledo.

Here Colonel Moscardó had joined the rising, but had been unable to hold the city. Instead, he was besieged in the majestic fortress, the Alcázar, which enjoyed an almost impregnable defensive position, with

Internationalisation of the war

There were important political developments on both sides at the end of the summer. On

4 September a new Republican government
under Francisco Largo Caballero replaced Giral's
cabinet. Largo Caballero was a trade unionist,
the leading figure on the left of the Socialist
party, and identified with the revolutionary
insurrection of October 1934. Many saw him
as 'the Spanish Lenin'. He was able to
construct a cabinet of six Socialists – including
the moderates Prieto and Negrín, four
Republicans, two Communists, one Catalan
and one Basque Nationalist. He became
Minister of War as well as Prime Minister.

Largo Caballero's cabinet was much more
representative of the range of people actually
fighting for the Republic than Giral's had
been. Only the Anarchists declined to
participate, although on 26 September they
joined the autonomous government of
Catalonia in an unprecedented decision for a
movement that opposed the very notion of
the state. On 4 November, the Anarchists
took the final step and joined Largo

Francisco Largo Caballero with Republican soldiers and
volunteers, 29 July 1936. As Minister of Labour in the
provisional government in 1931, Largo Caballero had
issued decrees to help urban and rural labourers. He was
Prime Minister from September 1936 to May 1937, when
Communist opposition helped remove him from power.
(Topham Picturepoint)

Caballero's second cabinet. Although
Anarchist participation did not last many
months, until the very end of the war the
Republic had a civilian government
composed of various political and trade
union forces of changing relative strength,
and Manuel Azaña remained in office as
President. It was essential to try to hold the
disparate groups together, and to present the
Republic internationally as a continuation of
the pre-war, democratic Republic.

By contrast, the military were obviously
dominant on the Nationalist side. Martial
law was immediately proclaimed wherever
the rising succeeded in July, and the military

Junta established by Mola in Burgos declared it for the whole country as early as 28 July. The fusion of military and political power, and the centralisation of both, were consummated on 29 September when his fellow-generals named Franco both Commander-in-Chief of all Nationalist forces, and head of government. From 1 October, Franco referred to himself as head of state, and although colleagues such as Mola and Cabanellas were displeased, there was nothing they could do.

Franco set up his government in Burgos, and his military headquarters in Salamanca, in the archbishop's palace. He became known as *Caudillo* (chief), and *Generalíssimo* (supreme general). From then on, there was no doubt about where ultimate control lay in Nationalist Spain, whereas on the Republican side control continued to be disputed, between the political parties, between the government and the revolutionary committees, and between Madrid and Barcelona. Largo Caballero moved to undermine one of the systems of dual power in October, when he decreed the incorporation of the militias into 'mixed

brigades' in the new Popular Army, but party and union affiliation remained the basis of many units.

The Republic was in urgent need of arms. The British and French policy of non-intervention resulted in the establishment of the Non-Intervention Committee, which first met in London on 9 September, and the Non-Intervention Agreement, by which signatories agreed to prohibit all exports of arms to Spain. By the end of August it had been signed by all the major powers, including Germany and Italy, which continued to supply Franco, and the Soviet Union, which was about to start supplying the Republic.

This charade of non-intervention was painful for the Republic. It became heavily dependent on Soviet arms, and through them on Soviet military and political advisers. Only Mexico sent arms openly to the Republic, on

General Franco, flanked by General Cavalcanti and General Mola, in Burgos on 1 October 1936. Franco had just been elected Commander-in-Chief and Head of Government by his fellow-generals. This combination of military and civil authority gave Franco unified control of all aspects of Nationalist Spain. (Topham Picturepoint)

Battles round Madrid, November 1936 – March 1937

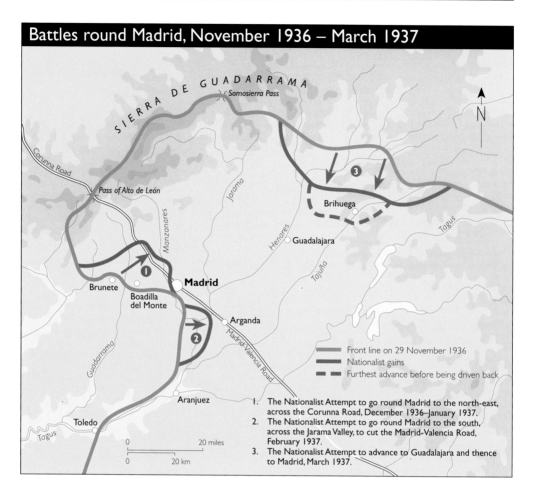

SIERRA DE GUADARRAMA

Somosierra Pass

Corunna Road

Pass of Alto de León

Jarama

Manzanares

Henares

3

Brihuega

Tagus

Guadalajara

Tajuña

1

Brunete

Boadilla
del Monte

Madrid

Arganda

Guadarrama

2

Madrid-Valencia Road

N

Aranjuez

Toledo

Tagus

0   20 miles

0   20 km

▬▬▬ Front line on 29 November 1936
▬▬▬ Nationalist gains
■ ■ ■ Furthest advance before being driven back

1. The Nationalist Attempt to go round Madrid to the north-east, across the Corunna Road, December 1936–January 1937.
2. The Nationalist Attempt to go round Madrid to the south, across the Jarama Valley, to cut the Madrid-Valencia Road, February 1937.
3. The Nationalist Attempt to advance to Guadalajara and thence to Madrid, March 1937.

a small scale. Otherwise, the Republic had no choice but to pay inflated prices for often sub-standard guns, ammunition and aeroplanes purchased on the black market in Paris, or Prague, or in the United States, in addition to paying over the odds for Soviet supplies. On 25 October Finance Minister Negrín shipped the gold reserves of the Bank of Spain to Moscow, as downpayment.

The first consignments of Soviet tanks, aircraft, armoured lorries, anti-aircraft guns and artillery were already in Spain. The Soviet biplane I-15 and monoplane I-16 fighters were new and fast, and flown by Soviet pilots. These fighter-planes, known in Spain respectively as *chato* (snub-nose) and *mosca* (fly), were supplemented by bombers. With about 100 aircraft in all, the Republic suddenly had the means to establish air superiority. Meanwhile, the Soviet T-26 tanks and

anti-aircraft guns were also superior to the German and Italian models in Spain, although this advantage would soon be challenged by the dispatch, in early November, of the German Condor Legion to Spain.

In addition to these crucial Soviet supplies, one other new resource arrived in time to participate in the defence of Madrid. The International Brigades were formed by the Comintern, from volunteers already fighting in Spain, not least from Italy and Germany, and from new volunteers flocking to Spain from right across Europe and beyond to fight fascism. Eventually about 35,000 men served in the International Brigades. Most but not all were Communists, the great majority were working-class men, and on 14 October the first 500 were brought to the base in Albacete, about 150 miles (240 km) south-east of Madrid, where André Marty, a top Comintern official, was commander. By the end of October, only those who chose not to see could deny that on both sides the Spanish Civil War had been internationalised.

The battle for Madrid

On 29 October the Nationalists began a heavy bombardment of Madrid, while the Army of Africa fought its way, village by village, to the south-west outskirts of the city, and seized the airport at Getafe on 4 November. By 6 November Varela's forces were right on the edge of Madrid. Meanwhile, Soviet planes went into action for the first time on 4 November, repulsing Junkers 52 bombers. The new tanks went into battle at the same time, and on 4 November the Anarchists entered the government.

Despite these positive developments, on 6 November the government, expecting an

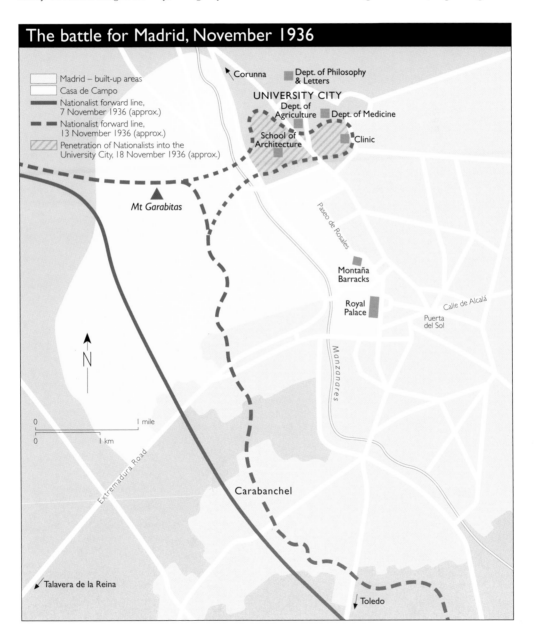

The battle for Madrid, November 1936

- Madrid – built-up areas
- Casa de Campo
- Nationalist forward line, 7 November 1936 (approx.)
- Nationalist forward line, 13 November 1936 (approx.)
- Penetration of Nationalists into the University City, 18 November 1936 (approx.)

Corunna

Dept. of Philosophy & Letters

UNIVERSITY CITY

Dept. of Agriculture   Dept. of Medicine

School of Architecture   Clinic

Mt Garabitas

Paseo de Rosales

Montaña Barracks

Royal Palace

Calle de Alcalá

Puerta del Sol

N

Manzanares

0   1 mile
0   1 km

Extremadura Road

Carabanchel

Talavera de la Reina

Toledo

General Francisco Franco, in 1936. Franco's military strategy was one of territorial reconquest. He was determined that bit by bit the whole of Spain would be under his control, even if this meant a long war of attrition. His terms for the end of the conflict were always unconditional surrender by the Republicans. (Topham Picturepoint)

imminent Nationalist assault, left Madrid for Valencia. General Miaja, commander of the Madrid military division, was placed in political as well as military control of the capital, with a political defence junta and Soviet military advisers to assist him. General Pozas continued in his post as commander of the Republican Army of the Centre, and General Rojo became chief of staff.

On 7 November Republican Mixed Brigades at last blocked the Nationalist forces advancing on west Madrid through the open ground of the Casa de Campo, preventing them from crossing the Manzanares river. The next day, three battalions of the first International

Brigade (the 11th Brigade) marched into Madrid and into history, cheered along the streets by desperate *Madrileños*. It was followed by another, the 12th Brigade, on 13 November. These international volunteers immediately contributed about 3,500 combatants to the defence of Madrid, but their effect on Republican morale was much greater. They gave new inspiration to the cries of 'They shall not pass' and 'Madrid will be the tomb of fascism', as the battle for Madrid was joined in earnest.

But in the high tension in the city, amid fears of both Nationalist victory and sabotage from a 'fifth column' of clandestine pro-Francoists, terror also continued. 'Political' prisoners held in the Model Prison and other Madrid prisons were evacuated from the capital under guard in double-decker buses on 7 November. They were deliberately massacred at Paracuellos de Jarama and Torrejón de Ardoz at the eastern approaches to the city, and their bodies dumped into mass graves. Between then and 4 December this outrage was repeated several times, and at Paracuellos and other sites at least 2,000 victims died, including 68 Augustinian monks from the community at El Escorial. This terror – the worst atrocity on the Republican side during the war – was ended by the Anarchist Melchor Rodríguez García, appointed as Director-General of Prisons on 4 December. Despite this humanitarian service, Rodríguez was sentenced to 30 years' imprisonment by a Nationalist military tribunal after the war.

If General Varela had taken Madrid, as he was widely expected to do, the blow to the Republic would have been immense, and possibly fatal. But on 9 November his attempt to penetrate Madrid through the working-class district of Carabanchel got bogged down, and the International Brigade launched a counter-attack across the Casa de Campo, at the horrendous cost of one in every three Brigaders being killed.

It was not until 13 November that Nationalist troops took Mount Garabitas in the north of the Casa de Campo, an excellent artillery position for attacking the city. And on 16 November the first Nationalist troops,

Moroccan Regulars and Foreign Legionaries, crossed the River Manzanares and fought their way into Madrid's University City. The opposing forces were strengthened by columns sent from Catalonia. In a grotesque parody of the usual purposes of the university, the School of Architecture and the clinic fell to the Nationalists, while Anarchists and International Brigaders held the Departments of Agriculture and Medicine, and after days of hand-to-hand fighting, Philosophy and Letters. Meanwhile, from 19 to 22 November, the Condor Legion subjected the citizens of Madrid to the most intensive aerial bombardment any city had ever known.

By 23 November both sides were exhausted, but determined not to relinquish what they held. Franco decided that Madrid could not be taken. His Republican opponents realised they could not dislodge the Nationalists from their present positions. The front lines stayed where they were, running through Carabanchel, the Casa de Campo and the University City, with trenches on both sides. Madrid stayed Republican, but under siege, at least to the west, for the rest of the war. The Anarchist leader Durruti was only the most famous of those who died in the battle for Madrid.

Madrid continued to suffer bombardment and artillery attack, and living conditions in the city deteriorated. But the collapse of civilian morale that the Nationalists hoped for did not occur. Franco's forces would have to go round Madrid, not through it. In December 1936 and January 1937 they tried the northern route, crossing the Madrid–Corunna road just north-west of Madrid, and pushing eastwards, but after initial advances they were driven back. The village of Boadilla del Monte was destroyed in the intense fighting, and both sides suffered many casualties.

The second attempt came in February, when the Nationalists under General Orgaz mounted a formidable onslaught to the south of Madrid, in the valley of the River Jarama. The aim this time was to reach and take control of the Madrid–Valencia road.

Once again, after initial success based on artillery superiority and the skill of the Moroccan Regulars, the Nationalist forces were repulsed. They gained some territory, but not their strategic objective. Joint action by the Republican armies of Madrid and of the Centre, Soviet planes and tanks, together with heroic resistance on exposed ground by Spanish and International Brigade soldiers, brought the Republic a costly but crucial defensive victory. Not for nothing did the British Battalion call one of the points they defended 'Suicide Hill'. Their commander, Tom Wintringham, recorded that almost two-thirds of the 600-strong battalion were either killed or wounded, among about 45,000 casualties on both sides. Jarama was also a ferocious first experience of war for the American Abraham Lincoln Battalion: 120 of its 450 men died.

The Málaga campaign

Round Madrid, defence rather than attack was prevailing. But this was not true of the other area of battle in January and February – the isolated coastal strip of Republican territory round Málaga. Here the task of the advancing Spanish and Italian troops proved relatively easy. The Duque de Sevilla approached Málaga from the west, and Colonel Muñoz from the north-east. On 5 February nine Italian battalions moved towards the city from the north. There was not much that Colonel Villalba, in charge of defending Málaga, could do. He lacked adequate arms, and Málaga could not be supplied from anywhere else. Refugees streamed east out of the city, along the coast road towards Almería. But the road was exposed to shelling from artillery and from Nationalist ships, and to air attack. Very many were killed. On 7 February Italian and Spanish troops marched into the city, and Mussolini claimed the first Italian victory of the war.

'Red' Málaga had been the scene of merciless vengeance on anyone identified with the right in July and August 1936. It was now the scene of unbounded retribution, as

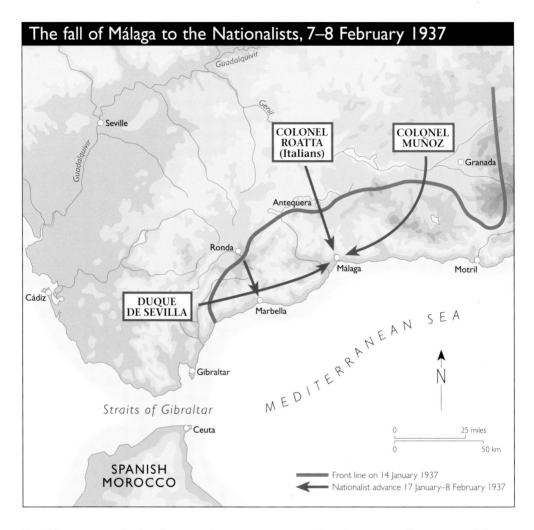

The fall of Málaga to the Nationalists, 7–8 February 1937

Republicans were seized and executed on a scale not experienced since Badajoz. The violence of the repression alarmed Italian leaders, just as the plight of those fleeing along the road to Almería appalled many observers. This was a civil war in which cruelty as well as heroism was commonplace, because each side loathed and feared everything that the other stood for.

A bizarre symbol of one of the different cultural worlds that the two sides broadly represented made an unexpected appearance in the Málaga campaign. Republicans had taken a preserved hand, venerated as a relic of St Teresa of Avila, from a convent near Ronda. It was found and sent to Franco himself, who kept it by him for the rest of the civil war, and indeed until his death in 1975, when it was returned to the convent. Franco regarded St Teresa, and Isabella of Castile, as the supreme embodiment of the true Spain he was rescuing from depravity and error.

Meanwhile, on 21 February, General Asensio was sacked from his post of Republican Under-Secretary of War. After the defeat at Málaga, Prime Minister Largo Caballero could no longer save him from Communist criticism. The war was taking its toll politically on the Republican government, and Communist influence was growing.

Guadalajara

Italian troops played a major part in the next Nationalist attempt to loosen the

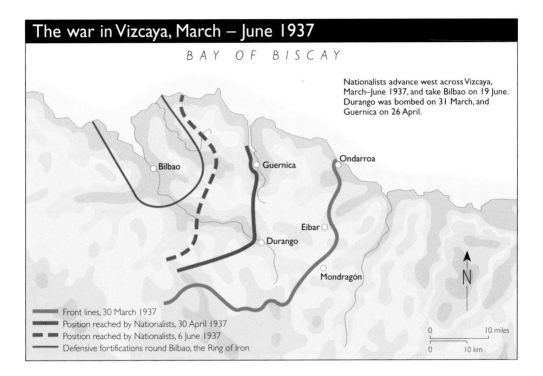

The war in Vizcaya, March – June 1937

BAY OF BISCAY

Nationalists advance west across Vizcaya,
March–June 1937, and take Bilbao on 19 June.
Durango was bombed on 31 March, and
Guernica on 26 April.

Bilbao   Guernica   Ondarroa

Eibar

Durango

Mondragón

N

- Front lines, 30 March 1937
- Position reached by Nationalists, 30 April 1937
- Position reached by Nationalists, 6 June 1937
- Defensive fortifications round Bilbao, the Ring of Iron

0   10 miles
0   10 km

Republicans' hold on Madrid. This time the focus was on the north-east approach to the city. Nationalist forces had won control of Sigüenza earlier in the war, but access to Madrid was blocked by Republican territory. In early March 1937 over 30,000 Italian soldiers, supported by tanks, artillery and 50 fighter-planes, joined forces with Moroccan and Carlist units at Sigüenza, with the aim of breaking through Republican lines and taking Guadalajara. This formidable concentration never got that far, but at first looked as though it would. Using what would soon be known as *blitzkrieg* tactics, they drove the Republicans back and seized Brihuega. But the advance got bogged down in the sleet and mud of heavy winter storms.

Republican forces, including Italian volunteers in the Garibaldi Battalion, regrouped, resisted and then counter-attacked. Once again, as in the battle for the Corunna road and the battle of Jarama, Nationalists gained small amounts of territory, but failed to achieve their objective. Guadalajara remained in Republican hands. The third and best-equipped attempt to encircle Madrid had collapsed.

Mussolini suffered the embarrassment of defeat, exacerbated by the fact that his Italian conscripts had fought against Italian volunteers in Spain and lost. Thousands of his men had been killed or wounded, large quantities of arms, including armoured vehicles, had been captured, and the whole world now knew for sure that fascist Italy had committed enormous resources, ineffectively, to Franco's cause. Chagrin and rage in Rome were matched by relief and jubilation in Madrid. The Nationalists decided that an attacking strategy around Madrid was ineffective and costly. Action now moved away from the capital to the northern front.

The Vizcaya campaign

In the spring of 1937 the main focus of the war was the Basque province of Vizcaya. Together with Guipúzcoa and Alava, it had committed itself to home rule during the Republican years, and the Basque Nationalist Party (PNV) had attempted to gain an autonomy statute for the whole area from Madrid – an issue that was still under discussion when the war broke out. The Basque country was one of the most fervently Catholic parts of Spain, yet the PNV's passion for Basque autonomy, and dislike of militarism, kept the two coastal provinces and part of Alava on the Republican side of the civil war in July 1936, to the scandalised amazement of many Catholics elsewhere in Spain.

Once the war began, the autonomy issue was speeded up, and on 7 October the first Basque government, led by José Antonio Aguirre, took office in the new autonomous region of Euzkadi. By this time, however, its claimed territories were already severely diminished. Much of Alava had fallen immediately to the rebels in July, and the Nationalists had taken Irún, on the French border, from its Basque defenders on

General Franco with Colonel Moscardó and General Varela, at the Alcázar in Toledo, 29 September 1936. Franco's decision to relieve the siege of the Alcázar rather than head past it for Madrid, gave the Republic precious extra time to prepare the defence of the capital. But it was politically astute, and Moscardó, hero of the siege, became a major figure in Nationalist propaganda. (Topham Picturepoint)

4 September, severing communications between the Republic and France along the north coast. Worse still, Guipúzcoa's capital, San Sebastián, was surrendered to General Mola on 13 September, and with it the rest of the province. As Nationalist forces advanced across Guipúzcoa, they executed 14 Basque priests and imprisoned many more for political deviancy: that is, sympathy with Basque nationalism. It was extraordinary behaviour for military authorities fighting – as they claimed to do – for the restoration of religion.

After the fall of Guipúzcoa, only Vizcaya remained, with its capital, Bilbao, and its powerful concentration of iron mines, steel works, shipbuilding and engineering companies – the very heart of Spanish heavy industry. Round the city, its defenders had built fortifications, a 'ring of iron' that curved from the coast, west of the River Nervión, about 15 miles (24 km) inland, south of Bilbao, and back to the coast further east along the Bay of Biscay. The Basque government had about 30,000 men in arms, but few ships to counter the growing Nationalist fleet, and only a small number of planes. Relations internally between the

General Franco with General Wilhelm Faupel, the Nazi regime's representative to the Nationalist government, 9 March 1937. Franco depended heavily on Nazi planes, bombs, and tanks, but was wary of Faupel's political sympathies with the Falange. The unification of all Spanish political forces into one movement in April 1937 brought the Falange under his direct control. (Topham Picturepoint)

The Basque town of Guernica after it was bombed by the Condor Legion on 26 April 1937. It became an international symbol of the inhumanity of modern war when Picasso painted his huge *Guernica*, now in the Reina Sofía gallery in Madrid, for the International Exhibition in Paris in 1937. (Topham Picturepoint)

dominant Basque Nationalists and their
Socialist and Communist colleagues were
difficult, and communications with the main
Republican army of the North under General
Llano de la Encomienda back west along the
coast at Santander were poor. The Nationalist
forces on the Vizcaya–Alava border also
numbered approximately 30,000, but were
backed by the Condor Legion and Italian
and Spanish planes – about 150 in all.

On 31 March Mola began the campaign
in Vizcaya by bombing and machine-
gunning the town of Durango with Condor
Legion Junkers 52s. It was a road and rail
junction, but not a military centre, and the
250 people who died were civilians. This
terror from the skies was worse than what
Madrid had experienced, because Durango
had no defences. Mola's forces advanced
slowly, and a Nationalist naval blockade was
set up at the mouth of the Nervión. On
20 April, Mola's offensive resumed, and
Basque forces were driven further back.

On the 26th the country town of Guernica,
20 miles (32 km) from Bilbao, and the
traditional centre of Basque rights and
liberties, suffered the same fate as Durango. It
had no air defences. In the middle of the
afternoon, it was bombed and fire-bombed by

Nationalist forces marching through Bilbao after it fell on
19 June 1937. The fall of the Republican northern front
meant the end of Basque autonomy until after Franco's
death. Franco was particularly incensed that the Catholic
Basque Nationalist Party had fought against him.
(Topham Picturepoint)

several waves of Condor Legion Heinkel 111s
and Junkers 52s, together with Heinkel 51 and
Messerschmitt BF-109 fighters, which
machine-gunned the fleeing population.
The town centre was destroyed, and up to
1,000 people killed.

The Nationalists took Durango on 28 April
and Guernica on the 29th. They had earned
themselves a place in history as the first
forces to use massive bombardment of
civilian populations who had no means of
protecting themselves. For decades after the
war, the Franco regime added insult to injury
by denying that these towns had been
bombed at all, alleging that retreating
defenders had burnt them down. But Picasso's
1937 painting *Guernica* ensured that the
name of this Basque town, of about 7,000
inhabitants, would become world famous as a
symbol of the horror of modern war.

In May 1937 as Nationalist forces closed in
towards the 'ring of iron', Republican planes
were sent to help defend Bilbao, but a mass

evacuation of Basque children to France, Britain and the Soviet Union underlined the gravity of the situation. On 3 June General Mola died when his aeroplane crashed, and he was succeeded as commander of the Nationalist Army of the North by General Dávila. The Nationalist advance resumed on 11 June. The next day the 'ring of iron' was penetrated. As civilians streamed westwards along the coast to Santander, they were strafed from the air just as refugees from Málaga had been. On 19 June the Nationalists entered Bilbao. Euzkadi's brief existence was over. Autonomy was dead. Basque iron, steel and chemicals were now at the disposal of the Nationalists.

Nationalist advances

By the end of June 1937 it was evident that the Nationalists were steadily conquering Republican territory, in a bitter war of attrition. It was also ever clearer that Nationalist Spain was Franco Spain. In April 1937 Franco quelled the claims of Falangists and Carlists to separate political identities by decreeing the unification of all political forces, under his leadership. Monarchist traditionalists and revolutionary fascists suddenly found themselves unwillingly incorporated, with everyone else, into one movement, called FET y de las JONS (that is, the Spanish Falange with Carlists and National Syndicalists), which Spaniards soon learned to call simply 'the Movement'. Symbols too were commandeered from all sides – the red beret of the Carlists, the blue shirts and fascist salute of the Falange, the religious images venerated by Catholics – and made into the public face of Francoism.

In Republican Spain, such enforced unity was much more difficult. In May 1937 simmering opposition between the pro-revolutionary Anarchists, POUM, and left-Socialists on the one hand, and on the other the Communists and right-Socialists who put organisation for war above all else, erupted

A Nationalist soldier holds a cross. Many of those fighting on Franco's side saw the war as a religious crusade against atheistic Communism. This was especially true of the Navarrese Carlists who joined the crusade with enthusiasm. (Topham Picturepoint)

Junkers 87 (Stukas) on the Brunete front. The town of Brunete was virtually destroyed in the war, as Republican and Nationalist armies fought to control the approach to Madrid from the south-west. As in other battles around Madrid, there were heavy casualties for small, but crucial, territorial gains. (Topham Picturepoint)

April 1937. A university building in Madrid, shattered by shells. After hand-to-hand fighting in Madrid's University City in November 1936, the front stabilized there for the rest of the war. (Topham Picturepoint)

into a civil war within the civil war on the streets of Barcelona. The Anarchists were defeated and the POUM was destroyed. The POUM leader Andrés Nin was tortured and executed while in Communist custody. Prime Minister Largo Caballero, who had stood out against Communist and more particularly Soviet pressure for months, was forced to resign.

His successor, Dr Juan Negrín, a brilliant research physiologist and reformist Socialist, acknowledged the now overwhelming reliance of the Republic on Soviet military aid. His premiership endured until the last days of the war, and he achieved unity of a kind, but only by alienating all those who believed that the defence of the Republic counted for little once the revolution had been disowned.

Communist military leadership was much in evidence when the Republicans at last launched an offensive, in July 1937, to the west of Madrid, at Brunete. The forces under General Miaja numbered about 85,000 men, and included as many as 300 planes and 130 tanks. The plan was to take some pressure off the northern front, and to seize control of territory held by the Nationalists, thereby preventing reinforcements and supplies from reaching Nationalist troops besieging the capital. On 6 July Enrique Líster's 11th Division led the attack, and took the village of Brunete from the north. In the following days, neighbouring villages including Quijorna also fell to the Republicans, in heavy fighting in hot and arid conditions.

Nationalist forces were rushed to the spot, and the Republican advance was halted about 8 miles (13 km) south of where it had begun. On 18 July the first anniversary of the start of the war, Nationalist troops counter-attacked, helped by the new Messerschmitt fighters and Heinkel 111s of the Condor Legion, which from now on proved more than a match for the Republican air force. A week later, what was left of Brunete was back in Nationalist hands, while the Republicans retained control of other villages nearby, and the front was re-established, only about 4 miles (6.4 km) south of where it had been at the beginning of the month.

Like the Nationalists at Jarama and Guadalajara, the Republicans found at Brunete that a decisive attacking campaign round Madrid was beyond their capabilities. About 3,000 men died in heavy fighting in punishing heat, while thousands more were injured, and

BELOW Brunete, May 2001. The Franco regime re-built the church and town square in Brunete as they had been before the war, in a characteristic determination to return Spain to its earlier traditions. (Author's collection)

enormous quantities of arms were lost. Both sides killed prisoners of war taken in battle. Brunete itself was virtually destroyed. Franco later rebuilt its church and arcaded square exactly as they had originally been, in a symbolic restoration of traditional Spain. But these villages west of Madrid, where so many men, including the young poet Julian Bell, died, are now full of new housing developments for the Madrid middle classes, and the horrors of the civil war seem expunged from memory.

After this costly diversion at Brunete, the Nationalists returned in mid-August to the interrupted task of conquering the remaining Republican territories along the north coast. Moving east from Vizcaya and north over the Cantabrian hills into the province of Santander, the well-equipped army of about 90,000 men, more than a quarter of them Italians, overwhelmed their dispirited and disunited Republican opponents. Basque units laid down their arms as the Italians took Laredo on 25 August and Santoña on the 26th, but Basque faith in a negotiated separate deal was cruelly shattered when Franco repudiated the agreement that Italian commanders had made with Basque leaders. There was to be no special exemption for Basque soldiers' and politicians from the fate suffered by Republicans from Cantabria and so many other areas that fell to the Nationalists during the war.

The desperate wait on the quay for a rescue that never happened, imprisonment, and in some cases summary trial and execution, ended both the Basque soldiers defence of the Republic and the brief dream of an autonomous Euzkadi. Meanwhile, on 26 August, General Dávila entered the city of Santander, virtually without resistance. Trapped between the advancing Nationalists and the Bay of Biscay, tens of thousands of men were taken prisoner in the Santander campaign. Among those who escaped by boat from Santander was José Antonio Aguirre, President of Euzkadi.

A few days later, on 1 September, General Dávila began the final stage of the northern campaign, the conquest of Asturias. At first the Asturian forces, perhaps buoyed by defiant

Young victims of Nationalist bombing. The Republicans attempted to shock foreign governments into protest at the Nationalist bombing of civilians, including children. (Topham Picturepoint)

declarations of Asturian independence, and certainly helped by mountainous terrain, put up some weeks of stout resistance. But in mid-October German carpet-bombing and steady Nationalist advance on the ground broke the defence. Asturias repeated the experience of Santander, with military collapse, escape by sea for the lucky few, capture and summary justice for the rest.

Apart from some Republican soldiers hiding out in the Cantabrian hills, the whole of northern Spain was now controlled by the Nationalists. The war there was over. The great coal mines of Asturias, site and symbol of the 1934 revolution, now joined the iron and steel mills and shipyards of Vizcaya, as Nationalist resources. Inexorably, the balance of land, population and industrial and military production tipped in Franco's favour. He held two-thirds of the country. By the late autumn of 1937, it already looked as though his victory was only a matter of time. But both sides were now thoroughly organised for war, and well over one million men were under arms. The way to victory and defeat was going to be slow and deadly.

Teruel

The Republicans were first to launch a new offensive, at Teruel, in southern Aragón, on 15 December. Aragón had already seen action in late August, when the Republicans took the small but heavily defended town of Belchite, south and a little east of Saragossa, at enormous cost. They failed to get much further, and failed too in their aim of diverting Nationalist forces away from the northern campaign.

Earlier in August the Republican government had decided to dismantle the Council of Aragón as part of a drive to suppress the Anarchists and their collectivist revolution. But it was dangerous to move

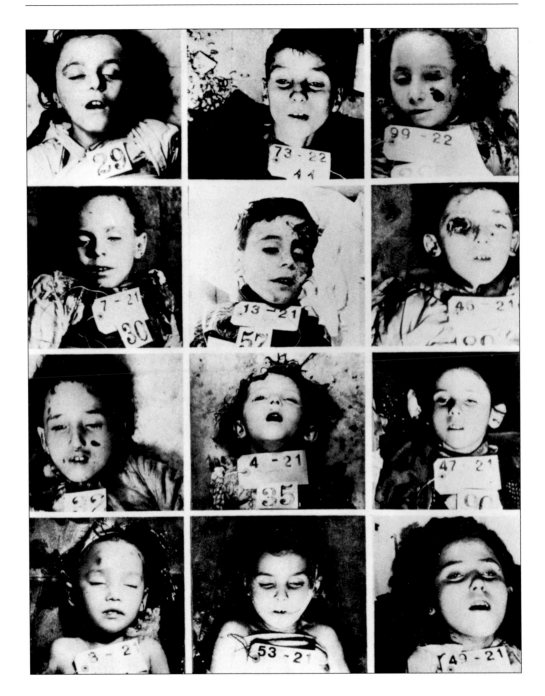

against revolutionaries while simultaneously expecting them to continue fighting. On the other hand, Prime Minister Negrín, Prieto and the Communists were all determined to forge a Republican army capable of defeating the Nationalists and not distracted by internal political disagreements. It was a dilemma without solution.

Against this very recent background of bitter political confrontation, and very limited military success at Belchite, the Republic launched its attack on Teruel in cold weather, with snow falling, and gained possession of most of the town. Rather than let a provincial capital fall into the hands of his enemies, Franco organised a counter-attack, but at first

A Republican soldier turns to face his pursuers. In the Spanish Civil War, the modern technologies of tanks and aeroplanes co-existed with very direct and personal combat on foot. (Topham Picturepoint)

it got held up in winter conditions. The Nationalist garrison in Teruel eventually surrendered, but the victorious Republicans were in turn besieged when the Nationalists outside the city were able to advance again.

By the end of February 1938 Teruel was back in Nationalist hands, after intensive fighting. Both sides had lost thousands of men. Moreover, whereas at the battles of Brunete and Guadalajara the side taking the initiative had advanced, and then been pushed back part of the distance it had gained, at Teruel the Republicans ended up in a worse position than where they started. Their bold initiative had proved counterproductive.

The Nationalists' eastern front stretched from the Pyrenees almost due south to just beyond the newly recaptured Teruel. In a series of campaigns in March and April 1938 it moved east until it reached, and in some places entered, Catalonia. The Republican army, battered by stronger forces with superior artillery and air power, and rent by internal political disagreements and failing morale, ceded control of what had been the revolutionary heartlands of Aragón.

The Nationalists swept as much as 70 miles (110 km) east in some sections of the front. On 10 March the already ruined Belchite was retaken. On 23 March Yagüe crossed the mighty Ebro river at Pina, south-east of Saragossa, gaining access to the main road east to the Catalan border and the city of Lérida, which capitulated on 3 April. And on 14 April Colonel Camilo Alonso Vega reached the Mediterranean at the fishing village of Vinaroz, cutting the Republic in two. His men celebrated a highly significant achievement, but for their opponents it was a bitter anniversary of the joyous proclamation of the Second Republic on 14 April 1931. Within a few days, the Nationalists controlled 40 miles (64 km) of the Mediterranean coast in the province of Castellón, in the region of Valencia.

After the collapse of the Republic's Aragón front, Franco was faced with the strategic decision of moving first against Catalonia, or turning south and west. He chose the latter. Between late April and the end of July, the Nationalist army edged its way down the Mediterranean coast, taking Castellón, and also mopping up the hinterland. Progress was slow and costly in casualties, and it proved impossible to dislodge the well-prepared defenders of the city of Valencia. The Republic's position was clearly perilous, but it still had men, and it received new equipment from the Soviet Union and across the briefly reopened French frontier.

Crucially, continuing the fight seemed to many preferable to unconditional surrender, which was the only alternative Franco would contemplate. In the tense international situation of the summer and autumn of 1938, Negrín hoped that if only the Republic could hold on, its troubles would be gathered into and transformed by the greater European war that he saw looming. This was the context for the last great Republican offensive, the battle of the Ebro.

The Ebro offensive

The southern reaches of the Ebro river from below Lérida to the Mediterranean had become the new demarcation line between Nationalists and Republicans after the fall of Aragón. The Ebro was a great natural barrier. Republican strategists, however, planned an audacious crossing of initially about 80,000 men. The author of the plan was General Rojo, the Republican Chief of Staff, and the action would involve several of the Republic's outstanding military commanders, including Lieutenant-Colonel Juan Modesto, Enrique Líster, and the young Lieutenant-Colonel Manuel Tagüeña Lacorte. The strategic aim was to draw Nationalist troops away from their advance on Valencia, and perhaps even to reunite the two sections of the Republic. The territorial aim was to gain control of the town of Gandesa, to the west of the Ebro, because of its importance as a communications centre.

On the night of 24–25 July, Republican troops crossed the River Ebro at several points, using boats, rapidly assembled footbridges of hexagonal cork floats, and pontoons. They established bridgeheads on the west bank, and then continued on. This massive, carefully

The battle of the Ebro, July – November 1938

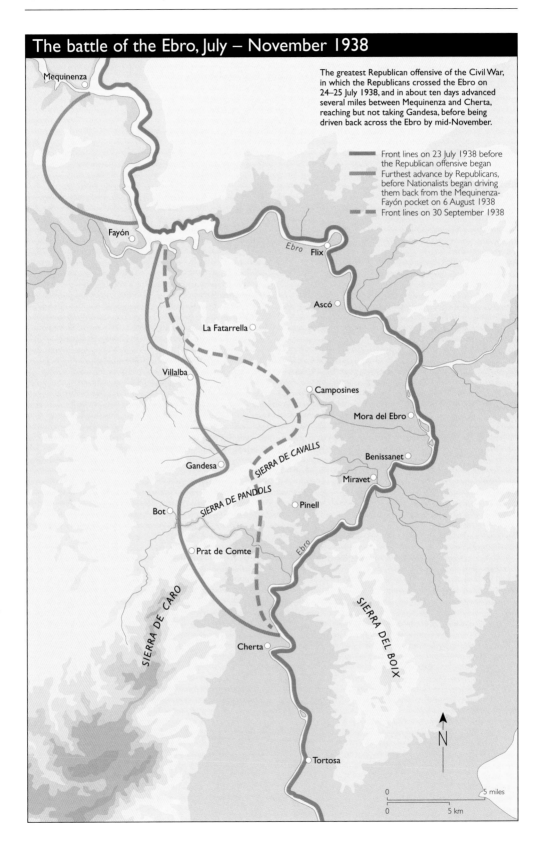

The greatest Republican offensive of the Civil War, in which the Republicans crossed the Ebro on 24–25 July 1938, and in about ten days advanced several miles between Mequinenza and Cherta, reaching but not taking Gandesa, before being driven back across the Ebro by mid-November.

Front lines on 23 July 1938 before the Republican offensive began

Furthest advance by Republicans, before Nationalists began driving them back from the Mequinenza-Fayón pocket on 6 August 1938

Front lines on 30 September 1938

Mequinenza

Fayón

Ebro Flix

Ascó

La Fatarrella

Villalba

Camposines

Mora del Ebro

Benissanet

Gandesa

SIERRA DE CAVALLS

Miravet

SIERRA DE PANDOLS

Bot

Pinell

Prat de Comte

Ebro

SIERRA DE CARO

SIERRA DEL BOIX

Cherta

N

Tortosa

| 0 | | 5 miles |
| 0 | 5 km | |

orchestrated initiative took their opponents by surprise, although they soon deployed air and artillery power against the advancing forces, and severely impeded the transport of armour across the river. Within a few days, Republican troops had advanced several miles west, establishing a new front between Mequinenza and Cherta, and capturing Nationalist soldiers who were surrounded. Other Nationalists fell back on Gandesa. It was a great victory, and persuaded many otherwise pessimistic Republicans that all was not lost. It was certainly cause for celebration.

As so often in the Spanish Civil War, however, it soon proved hard to exploit the initial advance. Crucially, the attempt to take the town of Gandesa failed. But controlling Gandesa was the essential element for the success of the rest of the campaign. Fiercely as

the Republicans advanced against its defences, they could not prevail. As Franco ordered several divisions and virtually the whole of the air force to the area, the Republicans dug in.

It took the Nationalists three and a half months to recover what the Republicans had taken in a few days. As early as 6 August, the Nationalists retook the northern section between Mequinenza and Fayón with heavy artillery fire followed up by the infantry. Bit by bit the Republicans were forced back, in burning summer heat, suffering constant aerial bombardment. By the end of September they had lost about one-third of the initial gain. From the end of October to 16 November, Franco pounded the Republicans from the air and from artillery batteries, before sending troops to wrest territory from them, mile by mile, settlement by settlement. By mid-

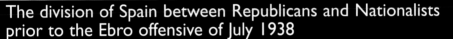

The division of Spain between Republicans and Nationalists prior to the Ebro offensive of July 1938

November the Republicans had retreated back across the Ebro, in good order, but defeated.

The last major Republican offensive, and the greatest battle of the civil war, was over. There were almost 100,000 casualties. It was also the last engagement of the International Brigades, which were disbanded in November 1938, partly because by this stage they were largely composed of Spaniards anyway, and partly in a vain attempt by Negrín to achieve the withdrawal of all foreign participants on both sides. Meanwhile the Nationalist armies engaged in the Ebro campaign, plus those of the centre and the south, now numbered over one million men.

The two great Nationalist targets remained what they had always been – Madrid and Barcelona. These now looked very vulnerable, as all the indicators – men, material, food, economic production, territory – pointed to ever-greater dominance by the Francoists. Living conditions in both cities were appalling. In Barcelona they were to deteriorate further once the Nationalist campaign to take Catalonia began on 23 December. Three different advances from the Ebro towards the coast, to Gerona, Barcelona and Tarragona respectively, met with very little resistance from demoralised troops. By 14 January Yagüe was at Tarragona, and on 26 January Barcelona fell, as soldiers and civilian streamed north to try to escape over the French frontier.

Between 27 January and 10 February over 400,000 refugees sought shelter in France, but found themselves without protection against wind and cold, herded into makeshift open camps on the beaches, surrounded by barbed wire, with no sanitation and at first no food. Members of the Catalan and central governments, including President Manuel Azaña, crossed the frontier, now refugees themselves. It was a tragic end for several different dreams: of a democratic Spain, of an autonomous Catalonia, and of a revolutionary, egalitarian, atheistic Utopia.

The Republicans still held almost a third of the Spanish land mass, including Madrid, and there were half a million soldiers in the Republican army of the centre, under Miaja. Prime Minister Negrín, other cabinet members and many army officers returned to Spain to continue the war. But victory was impossible. On 27 February Britain and France recognised Franco's government. On the 28th Azaña resigned as President of the Republic. The fighting was not yet over, but the outcome of the war was clear.

Crossing the Ebro, 24–25 July 1938. The greatest Republican campaign of the war, the Ebro offensive was a triumph of logistical planning, co-ordination, and engineering. Thousands of soldiers crossed the River Ebro on cork floats and pontoons, and swept through Nationalist territory before being stopped and then gradually driven back. (Aisa)

Front line volunteers

In the early stages of the war, both sides were poorly organised, and in both there was a confusing mixture of regular soldiers, armed security forces and militias with limited or no military training. Regular soldiers wore the standard-issue greenish-khaki tunic, cap, trousers and brown boots of the prewar Spanish army, whichever side they ended up on. Especially in the first weeks and months of the war, it was easy to mistake the regular soldiers on both sides. Similarly, the Civil Guard had their distinctive green uniforms with black leather hats, the Assault Guards wore dark blue, and the carabineers pale green with a peaked cap.

Other forces existed only on one side. On Franco's side, the Spanish Foreign Legion wore grey-green, and the Moorish regulars wore khaki drill shirts, covered with a rough poncho in cold weather, baggy trousers and a brown turban and sometimes a red fez as well. The Foreign Legion and the Moorish forces often wore rope-soled canvas shoes, *alpargatas*, in the summer. The Falangists had dark blue or black caps, and blue shirts; the Carlists red berets, and khaki shirts and trousers, often with *alpargatas*. On the Republican side, workmen's overalls and shirts became the improvised uniform of the militias, first in denim blue, then dyed brown or khaki, given a military air by a cap. Gradually, a more military dress of trousers and shirt and jacket appeared. Both sides adopted whatever winter coats they could procure, including US army supplies, and both sides often lacked boots and socks.

Poor, old equipment, including rifles from the Spanish–American War of 1898, and pre-1914 bayonets, was common at the start. Food supplies were at first haphazard, then gradually regularised for both Nationalist and Republican troops, but there is no doubt that, as the war continued, the Nationalist armies were better fed than their opponents. They also had a steady supply of tobacco, from Morocco, which the Republicans lacked. Both sides had poor sanitary and washing conditions, and were plagued by lice.

José Durán

A sense of the chaos and the territorial extension of the war is given in the account of his war experiences by José Durán, of Jerez de la Frontera, in Cádiz province, where his father was a doctor. Immediately after the rising of 18 July, he joined the rebels, even though he was under age. He chose first the town Guards, but got bored with security duties that he was assigned. He enlisted with the Falange, and took part in the Nationalist attack on Málaga. He then decided to leave the front, trusting in the fact that he was still under age to save him from any repercussions. He simply did not like the officers of his unit.

Next, he headed for Cádiz, enlisted in the Nationalist army and went through a brief training course, from which he emerged a sergeant. His war itinerary then took him to Córdoba, and Talavera de la Reina. He transferred to a Navarrese unit because he heard that its arrangement for leave was generous, and was sent to the front at Guadalajara, after the Nationalist and Italian defeat. He eventually participated in the Ebro campaign, where he was in command of 500 men. He entered Barcelona with the triumphant Nationalists. His final posting was back in the south, in Murcia, where – now a lieutenant – he was instructed to take the Republican military command centre. Colonels of the Republican army surrendered to him, and he arrested them. In three years the war had taken him across half of Spain, and changed his status from that of a boy-volunteer to an experienced military officer. But his ability to leave the front and change units is a useful reminder of the confusion and lack of ordinary army discipline in the first months of the war.

Antonio Izu

There were many who had been waiting for the day to dawn when they could fight for the Spain of their desires. One example in Ronald Fraser's oral history of the Civil War, *Blood of Spain*, was Antonio Izu, from a Carlist village near Pamplona. His family of modestly prosperous peasant farmers had been Carlist for generations. On hearing of the military rising, he was happy. 'I didn't sleep all that night, thinking what a hell of a shindy we were going to kick up.' He immediately grabbed a rifle and joined the Carlist militia, the *requetés*. He and his companions were directed to march on Madrid, and headed for the Somosierra pass, north of the city, in the Guadarrama mountains. They wore *alpargatas*, and made do for several days with a cold diet of bread and sardines.

For them, the war was above all a religious crusade. Many Nationalists, but especially Carlists, wore badges of the Sacred Heart of Jesus stitched on to their uniforms over their hearts as a symbolic protection against enemy fire. These were called *detentes* because the soldiers said this prayer: 'Stop, bullet, the heart of Jesus is here.' But Antonio was appalled when he heard about the repression of leftists back in Pamplona, and sickened when his company commander, a Falangist officer, seized 13 poor peasants from a village near them at the front who had supported the Popular Front, and shot them.

They took the poorly defended pass fairly easily, then fought their way to control of several villages. Antonio was shocked at the near destitution he encountered in these villages. It was eye-opening to see the poverty from which so much support for the Republic's policies had sprung. Once they reached a point where enemy lines were strongly defended by artillery, they settled down and became part of the siege of Madrid. The enthusiasm with which Antonio had greeted the war did not last. He hated the amalgamation of the Carlists with the Falange in April 1937, and thought that Carlism's commitment to local liberties was betrayed by Franco's dictatorship.

Saturnino Carod

Saturnino Carod, also interviewed by Ronald Fraser, began the war as convinced of the importance of defending the Republic as Antonio Izu was about destroying it. He was the son of a poor agricultural labourer in Aragón, and had begun working at the age of six. As an adult, he joined the CNT and learned to read. Before the war Saturnino had become CNT regional propaganda secretary in Saragossa, preaching anarchism in the local villages. He escaped from Saragossa during the rising, and joined an Anarchist militia column fighting its way through Aragón back to the provincial capital. The column was poorly armed with whatever had been to hand – hunting rifles, shotguns, pistols and knives. It was undisciplined, but when he began to reorganise and militarise it, the peasants simply abandoned it. He eventually persuaded them to return, and to accept a fortnight's military instruction from loyal Civil Guards. He found it hard to persuade his column to dig trenches opposite the Nationalists' position at Belchite. His men wanted – suicidally – to advance, not dig in.

Saturnino was out of sympathy with the wave of collectivisations that swept over Aragón, because he knew how attached to their own small plots of land many peasants were. He nonetheless worked hard to make the collectivisation experiment a success. He understood the rage of many CNT members against the Spanish Communist party and its agrarian policies in 1937, and had to struggle to prevent his column from leaving the front to fight against the Communists in the rear. More and more he felt that the Communist forces at the front were being better equipped and armed than the Anarchists, and he recalled that at Teruel he was offered further arms supplies only on condition that he joined the party, which he refused.

At the end of the war, Saturnino was one of the thousands at the port in Alicante, waiting for ships that never came. He watched people round him committing suicide rather than be rounded up by the Nationalists. Yet by this stage he himself had decided that a Republican victory would have been fruitless because of the savage political conflicts between Republicans. He remained, however, a fervent anti-Francoist. After escaping from a prison camp in Spain, making his way to France and being held in a camp there, he embarked on clandestine CNT activity in postwar Spain. For this he was condemned to death, and served 18 years of a commuted sentence before being released in 1960. His extraordinary brand of idealism was one of the factors that kept the Republic fighting, yet in the end he was not convinced that the Republic represented him any more.

Jason Gurney

Among the approximately 35,000 volunteers in the International Brigades were about 2,000 from Britain. Jason Gurney's detailed memoir was published in 1974. He was a 26-year-old sculptor in Chelsea when he volunteered in December 1936. Like all International Brigaders, he was taken to the Brigades' centre at Albacete, where the men were issued with brownish shirts, trousers and jackets, some boots and a khaki beret.

They were harangued by the chief political commissar of the Brigades, André Marty, and eventually sent on to the British Battalion's training centre at the village of Madrigueras.

Coping with cold, winter rain and a poor diet was not easy, and the lack of tobacco made it worse. They had no rifles, and training was perfunctory. When eventually automatic weapons appeared, they were old, and with the exception of the reliable Maxims, did not work, or got jammed. Only the night before they left Madrigueras for the front south of Madrid, were they issued with poor-quality Soviet rifles. They were paid 10 pesetas a day. Of the 600 men with Jason Gurney, over half would be dead within weeks.

In February 1937 the British Battalion went into action as part of the XV International Brigade in the battle of Jarama, with the aim of preventing the Nationalists moving east and cutting the Madrid–Valencia road. The XV was a Mixed Brigade of infantry, artillery ('two old French 75s and one even more ancient English 5.2 Howitzer') and nine Soviet tanks. Different types of light automatics and rifles needed different ammunition. There was a babel of languages in the Brigade, making communication difficult at the best of times, and perilous in battle. They had no maps. They found themselves attempting to hold an exposed position against heavy artillery fire and a swift advance by experienced Moorish Regulars, whose speed and prowess were terrifying. They were overwhelmed. Jarama in the end was a success for the Republic because the Nationalists never got to the Madrid–Valencia road, and were driven back some way in a counter-offensive. But in 21 days, there were about 45,000 casualties. It was a soldier-intensive war.

Two Spains

As the Spanish Civil War progressed, it soon became clear that Republican Spain and Nationalist Spain were two different states, and even different worlds. The Republic remained under civilian government, which struggled to assert its authority. At first, it was powerless to restrain the social revolution that swept through the country when the war began. Then Largo Caballero's government of September 1936 to May 1937 had some success in containing the revolution, by bringing the Anarchists into government, subduing the revolutionary terror and building a new army that absorbed the popular militias.

His successor, Juan Negrín, backed by the Soviet Union and the Spanish Communists, went further and dismantled the revolution – ending the collectives, restoring private property and imposing political and military discipline in an all-out effort to concentrate resources on the military objective of fighting the war. But throughout the war, competing political parties and trade unions continued. Moreover, central government co-existed with autonomous regional governments. A Basque government exercised local power from September 1936 until the fall of Vizcaya in June 1937, and the Catalan Generalitat right up to the fall of Barcelona in January 1939. The Council of Aragón also claimed a quasi-governmental status until its dissolution by the central government in August 1937.

Nor was the government's authority helped by the fact that it moved twice under the pressure of Nationalist onslaughts. In November 1936 it abandoned Madrid for Valencia, and at the end of October 1937 it left Valencia for Barcelona, where relations with the Catalan government became particularly difficult. After the fall of Barcelona in January 1939, the Republic had no proper seat of government at all. But even at the height of Negrín's efforts, power was never fully centralised, and the pervasive influence of Soviet and Comintern advisers and the Communist Party was never fully accepted.

The contrast on the Nationalist side could hardly have been greater. Although political parties, notably the Falange and the Carlists, mobilised militias and other support, the dominance of the military was always obvious. It was generals who planned and led the rising against the Republic. In the summer of 1936, Mola controlled Nationalist territory in northern Spain, Queipo de Llano controlled Seville, and Franco controlled north Africa and the ever-expanding areas of southern Spain conquered by his campaign. Mola declared martial law – somewhat theoretically – over the whole country on 28 July 1936, and it was imposed in fact, wherever the Nationalists triumphed.

The first, rudimentary administration was set up in Burgos on 24 July by Mola, with General Cabanellas at its head. Franco was appointed head of government as well as Commander-in-Chief by his fellow generals at Burgos on 1 October 1936, and took to himself the title of head of state. He appointed a new provisional government on 2 October, and Burgos remained the centre of many government departments throughout the war, though some were located in Salamanca, where Franco established his military headquarters. In April 1937 he consolidated power further by unilaterally merging all political organisations in Nationalist Spain into one mass party. There could be no doubt that politics were subordinated to military needs, and Nationalist Spain was Franco Spain.

Whether Franco's Spain was fascist is more debatable. It adopted the fascist salute, but the traditional, red-and-gold monarchist flag. It was a one-party state, but that one party greatly disappointed the *camisas viejas*, the 'old shirts' of the earlier, radical stage of the Spanish Falange, as it became virtually an agency of the administration. Some fascist policies were borrowed directly from Mussolini's Italy, most obviously the Labour Charter of March 1938. A bureaucratic, vertical trade union was established, while all others were abolished.

In foreign policy, the early regime's sympathies were quite obviously with its backers, Nazi Germany and Fascist Italy. But in contrast to Hitler and Mussolini, the foundation of Franco's power lay in military victory, not mass mobilisation; unlike them he was first and foremost a soldier, and his own values remained those of the Spanish anti-democratic, military tradition. Furthermore, his regime handed to the Catholic Church a degree of control over education, culture, public morality, public spectacle and censorship that was unthinkable in Nazi Germany, and which even in Italy the church was struggling unsuccessfully to retain in the 1930s.

Daily life

Daily life as well as politics was very different in the two zones. On the Republican side, the first euphoria of social revolution in 1936 included the collectivisation of farms, especially in Aragón and Catalonia, and of industries and businesses, most notably in Barcelona. Workers took control, and the bourgeoisie seemed to disappear as proletarian forms of dress became the only safe ones apart from military uniform. Capitalism vanished. In some rural collectives, money itself was abolished.

It has always been hard to determine how successful the collectives were. They did not last long enough to provide much reliable evidence, since they were dismantled under government pressure after Largo Caballero's fall in May 1937. Moreover, the industrial collectives had to switch production to war needs, which made comparisons with previous output problematic. In agriculture, many peasants distrusted collectivism and would have much preferred the redistribution of land in individual plots. What is certain is that collectivisation made central co-ordination of war and other production extremely difficult. In the Republican economy as well as in politics, the dominant pattern in the first stages of the war was fragmentation.

As the war continued, and especially after Negrín became Prime Minister in May 1937, economic organisation lost its revolutionary features. But daily life was more and more dominated by the consequences of the Republic's military failures. As territory and with it the available population diminished, men were called up at ever-widening age extremes – eventually from 17-year-olds to 55-year-olds. Food supplies inevitably diminished. Queues for food became an inescapable feature of the war, and a black market with high prices developed. The population of Madrid had a particularly grim time. Not only had it somehow to endure siege and bombardment from November 1936 onwards, but over the last year of the war it also had to manage on a very meagre and inadequate diet. Rations of lentils became known resignedly as 'Dr Negrín's pills'.

By contrast, from the beginning the Nationalists held most of the great wheatlands of Old Castile, and as territorial dominance increased, a range of food including eggs, meat, oil, vegetables and rice was steadily available. Price controls were imposed on many basic foods, including wheat and sugar beet. Economic stability was aided by loans to the Nationalists – who had no gold reserves to fall back on – by sympathetic Spanish financiers, of whom the most important was the Catalan Juan March. Equally important was the willingness of big international companies like Texaco and Firestone to sell crucial commodities such as oil and rubber to the Franco regime on credit.

These arrangements, together with the systems agreed with Hitler and Mussolini for armaments, enabled the Nationalists to prosecute the war and take on the huge debts it entailed, amounting to about 700 million dollars by the end of the war, without having to tax the civilian population excessively. The Franco regime also confiscated the property of those it deemed politically responsible for provoking the rising of July 1936, or of sustaining the Republic after that date, a procedure governed by the notorious Law of Political Responsibilities of 9 February 1939. Thus history was rewritten, the rebels became the legitimate government, and the erstwhile legitimate political authorities of the Second Republic became rebels.

Nationalist Spain resounded with martial music, patriotic parades and Catholic hymns. It was always likely that the Catholic Church would be more sympathetic to a military regime of order and traditional values than to the secularising and modernising Republic. Many Catholics were deeply opposed to the Republic well before 1936. But for most of those whose minds were not already made up, the question of loyalties was settled irrevocably by the murderous anti-clericalism of the social revolution in the summer of 1936, in areas where the military rising failed. One side protected religion, the other attacked it and drove it underground. Churches were destroyed, religious symbols and statues defaced and smashed.

Almost inevitably in these circumstances, Nationalist Spain took on the mantle of a religious crusade. Priests blessed weapons, prayed that battles would go the right way and celebrated victory with religious services. In a famous joint letter of July 1937, the Spanish bishops argued that the war was a confrontation between Christian civilisation and atheistic Communism, and urged bishops all over the world to explain this to the faithful. Pope Pius XII could hardly avoid greeting Franco's ultimate victory with 'immense joy', in a radio broadcast in April 1939. A few church leaders had important reservations about the wisdom of siding so fully with one band against another in a civil conflict. Some prominent Catholic laymen pointed out that the violence against priests

and religion had been the policy of the revolutionary mobs, not the Republic itself. But the die was cast. Franco's Spain was Catholic Spain.

Women

The Nationalists were also traditionalists where gender roles in society were concerned. The Republic, on the other hand, represented change. One of the most famous Republican posters carried the slogan 'They shall not pass', which the great Communist leader and orator Dolores Ibárruri (*La Pasionaria*) had made into the rallying-call for the defence of the Republic, and especially of Madrid. Above this armed soldiers, one of them a woman, wearing the blue overalls that were the improvised uniform of the Republican militias in the early stages of the war, fired at their enemies.

Women soldiers and *La Pasionaria* became dominant images of the Republic at war. Women in unisex workers' overalls symbolised a new world, in which women and men could be equal. Women could be politicians, public speakers, even soldiers, the most traditionally masculine of all occupations. As it happens, the first British casualty of the civil war, the sculptor Felicia Browne, was killed in action in a Republican militia near Saragossa on 25 August 1936. Behind the lines, too, great changes occurred. The Second Republic had seen the entry of women into politics, as parliamentary deputies, voters and activists. Now the first female government minister was appointed, Federica Montseny, Anarchist Minister of Health in Largo Caballero's government in November 1936. At a less dramatic level, women on the Republican side took up work in factories and transport in unprecedented numbers, often directly replacing their husbands or brothers or fathers who had been called up to fight.

Of course, there were also common experiences across the two zones. Everywhere women suffered from violence, bereavement and hardship. Moreover, the exigencies of war itself created new roles for women, just as they had done in the Great War of 1914–18. Women took on the horrific duties of nursing seriously injured and dying soldiers on both sides, often in field hospitals that were themselves in danger of bombardment. The major Nationalist relief organisation, Social Aid, was largely the creation of a woman, Mercedes Sanz Bachiller, and mobilised thousands of women who distributed food and organised orphanages, canteens and other welfare services. Social Aid lorries with bread supplies followed conquering Nationalist armies into what had been Republican strongholds. Women joined other voluntary relief agencies too.

There was even a major female political figure in the Nationalist camp, Pilar Primo de Rivera, sister of José Antonio, the founder of the Falange, and herself the founder of its women's section before the war. She was thrown into a particularly important role firstly by the fact that José Antonio was in prison in Republican Alicante when the war began, and then by his execution, which occurred in November 1936 although it was not publicly confirmed until much later. In her brother's absence, then death, then elevation to the status of revered martyr of the Nationalist cause, Pilar became a national figure, leading the women's section which, like the Falange itself, swelled into a mass organisation in the summer of 1936. When Franco unified all political groups in Nationalist Spain in April 1937, it became the official women's section of the emerging regime.

On the other side, the image of female emancipation projected by the Republic was itself somewhat misleading. Women soldiers made excellent propaganda in the early weeks of the war, as young women rushed to defend Madrid and Barcelona against the military rising. But as early as September 1936, Largo Caballero's government decreed the withdrawal of women from the front, amid controversy about their role there. As irregular militias were replaced by the new Mixed Brigades of the reorganised Republican army, so the irregular presence of

women at the front ended. It had been a feature of the urgency of the crisis rather than of any widespread view that soldiering was a proper activity for women.

Similarly, the extraordinary Dolores Ibárruri, member of the Central Committee of the PCE, galvanised the Anti-Fascist Women's Organisation, but insisted that its role was at the home front, not the battle front. Moreover, everything had to be subordinated to the war effort. She had little sympathy with the conviction of the Anarchist association Free Women, that their campaign for women's equality could continue even during the war.

Nonetheless, the difference between the two warring sides as far as gender roles were concerned was profound. Pilar Primo de Rivera became a major public figure in Nationalist Spain, but she used that position to insist that women's overwhelming mission in life was motherhood and the domestic sphere. Women were men's nurturers and helpers, not their competitors or work colleagues. The gender ideology of Franco's Spain was an extreme version of separate spheres, in which women were legally and culturally subordinate to men. Men were warriors, leaders, workers and providers. Women were destined to bear children and look after the family. During the war, they were expected to dress soberly (and certainly not in trousers), to wear little or no make-up, and to avoid public entertainment like the theatre or cinema.

Divorce, introduced by the Second Republic, was abolished by the Nationalists. The Labour Charter enacted by the Franco regime in March 1938, and modelled on Mussolini's legislation of the same name, promised to 'liberate' married women from paid work. As early as September 1936, educational legislation ended the 'immoral' practice of co-education, and established separate syllabuses as well as separate schools for boys and girls. The emancipatory reforms of the Second Republic were swept away.

By contrast, the Republic at war, in all its various strands – revolutionary, democratic, Communist – continued to represent equal rights for women and men. Federica Montseny and Dolores Ibárruri held positions of political power that were inconceivable in Franco's Spain. The wartime autonomous Catalan government legalised abortion. Young women could wear unisex overalls or culottes, and did so because they were practical for the new tasks they were undertaking. In gender as well as in other aspects of political ideology, it was evident that the two warring sides represented, and if victorious would construct, quite different societies.

Terror

On both sides, the Spanish Civil War was peculiarly destructive. About half a million people died, out of a population of 24 million. Whole towns and villages were virtually obliterated, like Brunete, west of Madrid, and Belchite, in Saragossa. Families were also destroyed, both by death and by political divisions that sometimes pitted brother against brother, and father against son. The economy, too, was devastated.

Distinctions between life at the front and life behind the lines were often blurred. Nowhere was safe. Both in large cities like Madrid and Barcelona, and small country towns like Guernica and Durango, Nationalist planes brought death and desolation in a way that foreshadowed the much larger-scale bombings of the Second World War. It is not surprising that when Pablo Picasso was asked to paint a picture for the Second Republic's stand at the International Exhibition in Paris in the summer of 1937, he chose to portray the human tragedy of Guernica, destroyed in April 1937 by the Condor Legion, rather than military confrontation in battle. *Guernica* depicted the shattered lives and bodies of women, children, men at work and animals. This was the new reality of war. Civilians were also strafed from the air as they tried to move to safety. It was as dangerous to flee east from Málaga in February 1937 or west from Vizcaya in June, as it was to be a conscript at the front.

Most bombardment of civilians was done by the Nationalists, though the Republicans bombed cities held by their enemies, including Granada. The Nationalists also shelled and strafed civilians, as they took Republican territory and people fled rather than face retribution. But there was terror on both sides, especially in the early stages of the war, when there was no settled authority and very little restraint. Marxist and Anarchist revolutionaries seized the opportunity to rid the world of priests and the social elites, just as ruthlessly as Falangists, Carlists and army generals purged it of intellectuals, Republican politicians and town councillors, and trade union officials.

To be caught in the wrong place behind the lines in the summer of 1936 was a death warrant without appeal. Violence was widespread, ideologically driven and vicious. Extremists on left and right believed that the world could be reshaped by terror. The poet and playwright Federico García Lorca was arrested by the Falange on 16 August 1936 in his home city of Granada. He was executed on the morning of 18 August. García Lorca was 38 years old, an outstanding talent even in the glittering array of Spanish experimental writers of the 1920s and 1930s. He was not interested in partisan politics. But his homosexuality and his plays, with their critique of the stifling effects of Catholic, bourgeois conventions, attracted the hatred of the new masters of Granada. His fame proved no protection.

Similarly, many died at Republican hands for what they symbolised rather than for any political actions. In the orgy of anti-clerical violence in the summer of 1936, the thousands of victims included young novices who had not even begun a religious ministry, and individuals like Father José Gafo, a courageous, lifelong campaigner for social justice. They were killed just because of their identification with the Catholic Church. Neither youth nor commitment to social reform saved them.

As the war progressed and governmental authority was asserted in both parts of Spain, uncontrolled actions by zealots became less

Taking shelter in the underground, from Nationalist bombing. The population of Madrid, and later in the war, Barcelona, became accustomed to seeking refuge from aerial bombardment, an experience soon to be repeated in the Second World War by civilian populations across Europe and beyond. (Aisa)

frequent. Random arrests, and the dreaded *paseos* and *sacas*, in which prisoners were driven to a cemetery, or the verge of a country road, or a quiet spot outside a town, and shot, became less frequent. But the generals who had espoused violence in the first place when rising against the Republic showed few qualms in continuing to exercise it behind the lines as well as at the front. As the Nationalists occupied – or in their vocabulary, liberated – village after village, town after town, they brought with them bread and reprisals, even if the latter increasingly had a veneer of legality as peremptory military tribunals took over from sheer massacre.

On the Republican side, the popular tribunals that were established in September 1936 were an improvement on the frenzied vengeance of the summer, but they were a long way from representing the rule of law.

And even in the last stages of the war, moments of military and political crisis provoked vengeance killings, such as that of Bishop Polanco early in 1939, during the rout of Republican forces in Catalonia.

Republicans increasingly feared hidden enemies. The Spanish Civil War created the term 'fifth column', or at least gave it popular currency, when General Mola famously looked forward – in vain – to taking Madrid early in the war with four columns approaching it from outside while a fifth sprang up within. But a fifth column certainly developed in Madrid, which had to wait until March 1939 before it could declare itself, but which in the meantime engaged in clandestine activities of liaison and sabotage.

Undeclared Francoists existed everywhere on Republican territory, as they were bound to do, including at the front. It was in the nature of this war to trap large numbers of people on the 'wrong' side, in circumstances where they had little choice but to hide their opinions and participate in the war effort of their political enemies. From government and the top of the military command downwards, fear of disloyalty was pervasive.

Rumours of deliberate sabotage greeted every major Republican defeat.

Soviet advisers and Spanish Communist leaders were extremely sceptical about the reliability of Prime Minister Largo Caballero's Under-Secretary for War, General Asensio, and insisted on his removal from office after the fall of Málaga. He was later arrested on suspicion of treason after the fall of Gijón. He was a dramatic example of a widespread phenomenon. This was a war within one society, not between two different countries. Who was to say what identity a man or woman held in their heart? The enemy was not just on the other side. The enemy could be anywhere.

In Republican Spain, however, the enemy within did not have to be a 'fascist'. He or she might be a genuine supporter of the Republic, but out of step with the dominant interpretation of what the Republic should be like. From October 1936, when the Soviet Union came to the aid of the Republic, the influence of the Spanish Communist party, and more particularly of Stalin, the Comintern and the Soviet Union, grew ever stronger. Without Soviet supplies, the Republic could not have withstood the armies of Nationalist Spain, backed up by the Nazis and Fascists.

Communist exasperation with Largo Caballero was a major reason for his downfall as Prime Minister in May 1937, although many non-Communists also wanted him out of office. Similarly, Communist support for Juan Negrín, and his closeness, most of the time, to Soviet priorities in Spain, were essential factors sustaining his premiership from May 1937 until the last days of the war. Those priorities were straightforward. It was the policy of the Soviet Union, the PCE, a large section of the Socialist party and what remained of the left-Republicans to concentrate on the war effort, and to persuade the western democracies that this was a confrontation between a democratic regime and international fascism. Winning the war and drawing Britain and France into an alliance against Nazi Germany and Fascist Italy were the dual, and closely interrelated, aims.

There was no room in this agenda for the social revolution that Anarchists, the small anti-Stalinist Communist movement (the POUM) and left-Socialists launched in the early days and weeks of the war. George Orwell was exhilarated by his experience of revolutionary Barcelona in 1936, where a new, classless society seemed to be being created. Of course, conservatives, property-owners and Catholics feared the revolution. But so too did Communists and many others on the left who were aghast at what seemed to them irresponsible forgetfulness of the main priority, which was fighting fascism. Communist political commissars, secret police and political prisons set about imposing that priority in ways that earned the Communist movement the hatred and distrust of their rivals. The torture and killing of the POUM leader Andreu Nín while imprisoned by the Communists was a particularly vicious, but not unrepresentative instance of the political purge undertaken behind the Republican lines.

Long after the armed confrontation between the revolutionaries and their opponents in May 1937 in Barcelona, which the former lost, and the subsequent removal from government of Anarchist ministers, Communists continued to harry and repress those who did not accept PCE priorities and discipline. The Anarchist trade union organisation the CNT, which had been so dominant in Catalonia and Aragón in the first weeks of the war, was a much reduced and disaffected force in its later stages, as could be seen in the collapse of the Aragón front after the Ebro campaign, and the inability to defend Barcelona as the Nationalists approached. Ideological conflict weakened the Republic at war, and brought danger and death far behind the Republican lines.

Republican poster appealing to international opinion against the bombing of civilians in Madrid. Spanish and French versions of the poster were also issued. But the Republic's attempts to get the British and French governments to intervene in the Civil War failed. (Author's collection)

Culture

Both the strength of ideological commitment
and the problems it created were apparent in
one of the most notable artistic features of the
war – Republican poster art. The Nationalists
produced some posters too, but not on a
comparable scale, nor of such variety and
power. They did not need to. Military victory
was their greatest propaganda tool. Moreover,
the swift concentration of military and
governmental powers in Franco's hands at the
end of September 1936 enabled them to set
up a central propaganda office.

On the other side, however, political
parties and unions vied with one another to
get their particular message across. They
commissioned artists, especially in Barcelona,
to produce strong, vividly coloured posters
that could be printed in large numbers and
posted up on walls. They frequently featured
the initials, flags and other emblems of the
commissioning organisation in prominent
positions, while the artists' names were often
printed at the bottom or along the side.
Some posters displayed the hoped-for unity
of the Republic by depicting crowds bearing
the various flags of the Republican
movements – the red and yellow stripes of
Catalonia, the red and black of the
Anarchists, the red of the Communist Party.
The slogan of the 1934 revolution in
Asturias, 'Unite, Proletarian Brothers',
reappeared. Many posters pointed to the
shared hopes of freedom and victory, while
others brilliantly lampooned the combined
forces of money, fascism, armed might and
religion arrayed against the Republic.

A recurrent theme was that of foreign
invaders, German Nazis, Italian Fascists and
Moroccan soldiers, aiding the Republic's
enemies, especially before November 1936,
when the Republic itself still had no major
foreign assistance. But issues dear to the
particular commissioning organisation also
appeared. A powerful Anarchist poster, for
instance, depicted a rifle placed beside a
book, and claimed that the war against
fascism was also a war for literacy.
Communist posters emphasised the
importance of the popular front of all
Republican groups against the international
as well as national fascist enemy. There were
posters aimed at youth groups, at women, at
Basques, at peasants and at workers.

The Republic certainly needed to rally the
civilian population, and the quality and
artistic exuberance of many of the designs was
impressive. They belonged to, and extended, a
tradition of propagandist poster art going
back to the Russian revolution, and often
echoing the earlier iconography of the French
revolution. They lauded democracy, equality
and liberty. But the fact that they were
produced by so many different groups, and
expressed separate political priorities as well as
common aims, itself exemplified one of the
Republic's abiding problems. Passion and
diversity created dynamic visual art, but they
were hard to harness into a unified war effort.

'Until the end'. A poster issued by the POUM, the small, revolutionary, non-Stalinist Marxist party, urging Spaniards to persevere in the fight against Nazism. The POUM and their fellow-revolutionaries, the Anarchists, were overwhelmed by the Soviet-backed Spanish Communist Party, the PCE, during the war. (Author's collection)

Poster depicting the Republic, in the tradition of iconography made famous in the French Revolution. The plethora of flags surrounding the Republic showed its strength, representing Spain itself, Catalonia, and the working-class parties and trade unions. But this diversity was also an enormous problem for the Republic. (Author's collection)

'The cultural militias fight against fascism by combatting ignorance'. Poster issued by the Education Ministry of the Republic, juxtaposing a rifle with a school exercise-book, and arguing that the defence of the Republic would also promote popular education for the masses. (Author's collection)

Women and war: two memoirs

For some women, the Spanish Civil War was genuinely emancipatory. Young women on the Republican side joined trade unions, engaged in politics, took up all sorts of war work, and even briefly served as soldiers in the militias. The necessities of war and the outbreak of social revolution combined to open up these new roles. Even in the traditional culture of Nationalist Spain, young, middle-class, Catholic women found they could go out without chaperones, and many of them worked outside the home for the first time, supporting the war effort. Images of the Virgin Mary were everywhere in Nationalist Spain – in churches and homes, on banners, medals and schoolroom walls. She was honoured by Franco's armies, and was the crucial role model for women, who were expected to be devout and concern themselves with home and children. But the war needed women's participation as nurses, relief workers and secretaries as well.

For a third group of women, too, the Spanish Civil War presented new experiences. These were the foreign women who came to Spain. There were journalists, such as the American Martha Gellhorn, who began her career as a war correspondent there, and volunteers, like Nan Green, who left London for Spain to work as a medical administrator for the Republicans, or Thora Silverthorne from Wales, who nursed in operating theatres behind the Republican lines.

Sara Berenguer

Sara Berenguer was 17 years old when the Spanish Civil War began. Her memoirs were published in 1988. She was the eldest of five children in a working-class family that lived in the Las Corts area of Barcelona. Her father was a labour militant who had been in prison for his activities. Sara herself had gone to school only until she was 12, and had then become a seamstress. She had also attended a few typing classes. But in 1936 her greatest pride was her electric sewing machine.

The first she heard of the national crisis was when she was walking down the street to go to the beach on 19 July, and someone said, 'The revolution has begun.' Her father did not return home on the 19th or 20th, and had a gun when he briefly returned on the 21st, to prepare for the Aragón front. He took Sara to the revolutionary committee that had been established in Las Corts, and told them, 'My daughter wants to take part in the revolution.' The revolution is what she continued to call it, and her comment about that first involvement explains her own attitude very well: 'From that night on, I began to serve the cause of liberty.' She did a little guard duty in the neighbourhood, and then worked typing out guard rotas.

It is interesting that she was quite unfazed by the violent anti-clericalism that seized Barcelona. She recounts simply how she and a friend went out of curiosity to check what had happened to churches and convents, and 'to see the exhumed bodies of nuns in their shrouds' that the revolutionaries had torn out of their tombs and displayed in the street. Perhaps the message in this bizarre act was that there was no place now for convents and their alleged evils, or just that the revolutionaries were no longer bound by the usual norms of respect for the dead or for anyone else. Whatever it was, it did not dismay her.

A young woman collecting for the Nationalist armies in Salamanca in March 1937. But even in Nationalist Spain, women found themselves involved in helping the war effort in ways that were much less traditional than the one shown here. (Topham Picturepoint)

Similarly, she recalls quite dispassionately how she occasionally went alone to the local morgue in the morning, to see the one or two 'dead fascists' brought in each day after the previous night's killings.

One of the committee leaders told her to join a union, meaning by this one of the unions affiliated to the revolutionary Anarchist CNT, which was very strong in Barcelona. So little did she know about politics that at first she joined the textile section of the Socialist UGT. Her political understanding rapidly became more advanced as she spent her evenings at a centre for Anarchist youth. Meanwhile, signs of the new proletarian style were evident. Her father wrote to her mother asking for some socks, and for the first time ever, addressed her with the Anarchist term *compañera*. Her mother also made Sara the obligatory blue overalls.

For a while, Sara worked in the revolutionary committee's child-care centre, which had been taken over from nuns, and in which a few nuns, now in secular dress, continued to work. But she soon moved on to become the committee's secretary, receiving the same pay as everyone in the militias, 10 pesetas a day. She also gave classes to children, and attended further evening classes in typing, paid for by the committee.

Within days, Sara's life had been changed beyond recognition. She likened the revolution to a burst of light, which showed women a way forward that had been closed to them. She got home very late from the Anarchist centre. Some of her younger siblings were out all the time too. Young men and women began to have gym sessions together. Sara found herself involved in discussions about whether being a free woman meant being a sexual libertarian. To the disappointment of some of her male companions, she thought not. Couples began coming to the revolutionary committee to get married and acquire a marriage certificate. Religious marriage ceremonies, of course, were no longer possible. Anyway, the people she knew all hated priests. But, although things had changed and free love was being widely preached, many still wanted their relationships formalised.

Harsher realities of the war soon bore in, with her father's death at the front in October 1936, the first bombing raids on Barcelona in February 1937 and then the May days of 1937, when Communists and others opposed to social revolution fought on the streets of Barcelona with the Anarchists and the POUM. The building where she worked was later bombed. Meanwhile, she was drawn to the Anarchist feminist association *Mujeres Libres* (Free Women) because she was so angry when she saw young men laughing at a poster advertising a woman speaker at a *Mujeres Libres* meeting. The main focus of her activities, however, became the Catalan section of International Anti-Fascist Solidarity, which concentrated on social assistance and supporting men at the front. With Solidarity, she visited the front several times, and worked in an ambulance helping a nurse after bombardments.

Sara noted the general loss of earlier enthusiasm as the war dragged on. The Anarchist Youth organisation was weak in 1938, because even very young men of 17 were called up to fight. Women and children who were refugees from fighting elsewhere lived in awful conditions in Barcelona and other Catalan cities and towns. Sara represented Solidarity at the farewell ceremony for the International Brigades in Barcelona on 15 November 1938. The Brigaders were given a hero's farewell at this last parade, not least in *La Pasionaria*'s great valedictory speech, in which she declared, 'You are history. You are legend.' But the disbandment of the Brigades was another sign of how different things had become from the early months of enthusiasm.

At about the same time, Sara agreed to leave Solidarity for full-time work with *Mujeres Libres*, serving as Propaganda Secretary. She learned to give public talks, and to organise propaganda. But it was late for this. Barcelona fell to the Nationalists on 26 January 1939. Sara, like so many others, began the traipse to the frontier, and a lifetime of exile. The revolution had failed. She was still only 20 years old.

María Rosa Urraca Pastor

María Rosa Urraca Pastor was already a veteran of national politics when the Civil War began. She was a Margarita – that is, a member of the Carlist women's organisation – and was as completely committed to the Nationalists as Sara was to the Republic. Because María Rosa ended the war on the winning side, she was able to publish her war memoirs almost immediately. Her story could be told in Franco's Spain; Sara's could not.

María Rosa was Basque, but hated Basque Nationalism, and especially the decision of its leaders to side with the Republic in the war. In April 1931 she wept when the Second Republic was announced, and was soon involved in public demonstrations against its anti-clerical policies. She was fined the large sum of 500 pesetas in 1931 for promoting an unauthorised public meeting of women in the church of San Vicente, in Bilbao, to protest against the May church-burnings in Madrid. She became a skilled public speaker, and stood, unsuccessfully, for a seat in parliament at the general elections of November 1933.

María Rosa was obviously not a typical conservative woman. But she represents thousands of Spanish, middle-class women (her father was an army officer), who were politicised by the Second Republic. It is significant that before joining the Margaritas, she was involved in the women's section of Catholic Action, and that the 1931 protest was convened through Catholic Action, and took place in a church. The defence of religion and tradition was the central issue for many conservative women, who experienced the Republic as the imposition of an alien culture, in what María

Rosa herself called in a radio broadcast during the war, 'a shameful parenthesis'.

At the beginning of the Civil War, María Rosa went from Burgos to the Somosierra pass with the Nationalist forces, and spent a year at the front as a nurse. This was exceptional, a product of the first phase, when medical facilities were virtually nonexistent, and of her own determination. Other Margaritas, however, acted similarly if less dramatically as they took up work in hospitals, workshops and canteens. She left the Madrid area to accompany the Nationalist advance into her native Vizcaya, and was then appointed an administrator of the Nationalists' relief organisation, Aid to Fronts and Hospitals.

In her wartime talks and broadcasts, María Rosa argued that although she had been at the front, other women should not emulate her. She rejected the equality of the sexes, and argued that a woman's glory was to be a mother and the 'queen' of her own home. But she passionately wanted social justice for the poor, a classless society and national reconciliation after the war. The Franco regime espoused none of these.

Sara Berenguer and María Rosa Urraca Pastor were both exceptional women, but both also represented widely shared experiences of the Civil War. They knew its hardship and confusion. Their high ideals for a better society co-existed with dedication to political movements that were ruthless and vengeful. They belonged to different cultures and different value systems, and yet had much in common. María Rosa had worked to gain better conditions for female textile workers before the war. She and Sara both wanted better education for women. The fact that they were deeply committed to different sides, and that the victory of one was the tragedy of the other, is in microcosm the horror of the Spanish Civil War.

Franco's victory

Even after the collapse of Catalonia, Prime Minister Negrín was determined to fight on, still hoping against hope that the fortunes of the Republic would be transformed once a general European war broke out, in which the western democracies would at last have to confront Hitler's Germany. A number of military leaders, however, including Colonel Segismundo Casado, commander of the Republican Army of the Centre, thought that continuing the war at this point was simply irresponsible. In Madrid, food was scarce and living conditions were terrible. Morale in the Republican army was low. What was the point of more deaths?

Casado entered into negotiations with Franco's chief of intelligence in Burgos, Colonel Ungría, confident that some terms better than simple unconditional surrender could at this late stage still be achieved. He also began planning a coup against Negrín and his Communist backers. By early March, even General Miaja agreed with Casado's plans, and on 5 March Casado set up a so-called national council in Madrid and informed Negrín of his rebellion. Uncertainty and political confusion were rife, not just in Madrid, but throughout Republican Spain. No one was sure who had what authority, or who would follow any orders. Negrín gave up, and flew out of the country, accompanied by various Communist luminaries. But Communist army commanders in and around Madrid chose to attack Casado, and for one last, desperate time, there was a civil war within the civil war in Republican Spain.

By 12 March the Communist resistance had failed. Two of its leaders were executed, the latest Republicans to die in internecine disputes instead of in fighting the Nationalists. Others were imprisoned, and were still in gaol when the Nationalists entered Madrid. Casado discovered that his hopes of negotiating

anything with Franco were entirely groundless. The terms remained unconditional surrender.

In the south and the centre, Nationalist armies continued to advance while the opposing forces disintegrated. On Tuesday, 28 March, the Nationalists, headed by General Espinosa de los Monteros, entered Madrid. In the next few days, the scene was repeated in Valencia, Jaén, Almería and other southern cities. Fifth columnists emerged full of joy and relief to greet the Nationalist conquerors, and Nationalist flags appeared as if by magic on balconies. On 1 April, Franco issued the last communiqué of the war. 'Having captured and disarmed the red army, Nationalist troops today took their last objectives. The war is finished.'

Republican troops either melted away and headed for home, or found themselves rounded up in holding camps. Thousands of Republican activists made desperate attempts to leave the country. But they were unsuccessful. There could be no repetition of the huge exodus into France a few months earlier. The Republic now had no frontier with France or Portugal. Nationalist ships patrolled the Mediterranean, making escape by sea a forlorn hope for almost all of the up to 60,000 people thronging the docks of Alicante and other southern ports. Casado was one of the very few to be rescued. Some who found themselves trapped committed suicide rather than face the Francoist justice that was to come.

The fighting was over, but in some senses the war continued. Military justice officials were understandably keen to prosecute those suspected of participating in the Republican repression during the war. Anyone convicted of a 'crime of blood' of this kind could expect the death penalty. But the immediate postwar repression went much further than this. The rebel generals of 1936 saw themselves as opponents not just of the Second Republic as a constitutional and political system, but also of a

Franco - the victor of the Civil War, and dictator of Spain until his death in November 1975. Many monarchists and fascists in Spain were disappointed that he neither restored the monarchy after the war, nor fulfilled radical fascist aspirations. (Topham Picturepoint)

perverted ideology that they called 'red' or Communist. Throughout the war, the Nationalists called their opponents *los rojos*, 'the reds', just as the Republicans called theirs 'the fascists'. Neither label was accurate, but they summed up succinctly the sense among the deeply committed on each side that the other represented a completely unacceptable set of values.

The victors were now determined to create their own new but traditional Spain, and to eradicate 'red' Spain for ever. High-ranking army officers, and political and trade union leaders at national and local levels who had played a significant role in the Republican war effort, or who had participated in the Popular Front before the war broke out, were charged with treachery and military rebellion, even though it was their accusers and judges who had rebelled in 1936. They were brought before military courts. If they were found guilty – and the standards used to evaluate evidence were far from reassuring – they were executed or condemned to long terms of imprisonment. These sentences were punishment for individual actions that hindered the cause of

true Spain, as the judges saw it. They also regarded them as a way of purging the national body of corrupting influences.

Estimates of the numbers executed in the postwar repression have varied widely, but recent research, province by province, now points to a total of probably about 50,000. This figure does not include the many thousands killed in lawless reprisals in the early stages of the war, whose exact numbers will probably never be known. The new regime was not interested in reconciliation. It was interested in retribution, and in cutting out diseased members from Spanish society, lest they should infect others. The terminology of impurity and disease recorded the regime's view of Republican politics as pathological and contaminating.

Prisons were severely overcrowded, with over 200,000 inmates at the peak, in dire conditions, with inadequate food and little sanitation. Whole prisons were set up for women, and women were among those executed. The sheer scale of the prison population represented such a problem, even after executions had reduced the numbers, that from 1941 it was drastically diminished by widespread grants of parole and the commutation of sentences. There was no total amnesty for civil war actions, however, until 31 March 1969.

In addition to the prisons, work camps were established. The new regime used prison labour under military discipline, and with meagre rations, to rebuild towns, roads and railways. They were also put to work on other projects, including the enormous basilica hewn out of solid rock at the Valle de los Caídos, the Valley of the Fallen, near Philip II's Escorial palace, north-west of Madrid. This vast, ugly church became José Antonio Primo de Rivera's mausoleum, and ultimately Franco's. In Francoist discourse, prison labour was a way of permitting offenders to redeem themselves, a kind of penance that would fit them once more for membership of the national community. Many did not survive to see this benefit.

The Law of Political Responsibilities of 9 February 1939 made it a civil offence to have backed the Popular Front before the war, or impeded the Nationalists during it. This extraordinary, retrospective legislation was designed to enable the regime to confiscate property and impose fines on those who were found guilty, or if necessary their heirs. It permitted a massive forced transfer of property and resources from Republican organisations and individuals to Franco's state.

Republican supporters suffered in other ways too. Purge commissions were established for the professions, especially teaching, and for many other occupation groups. Anyone who did not meet the requirements of proven loyalty to the Nationalist movement (even from before it existed!) could be dismissed, demoted, barred from future promotion or relocated far from home. The purge commissions affected tens of thousands of people. They are perhaps the clearest example of the Franco regime's determination not just to punish its enemies, but to reshape Spanish society and culture. No one regarded as ideologically unreliable would be allowed to hold a position of responsibility or influence, or even, in many cases, to find employment at all.

Creating a new Spain that was authoritarian, anti-democratic, Catholic, conservative and anti-intellectual was facilitated by the tragic exodus of those who managed to get out. Soldiers, politicians, propagandists and trade unionists had streamed across the Catalan border into France in January and February. A whole generation of famous writers, poets, artists and musicians also left the country at the end of the war, including the composer Manuel de Falla, the poets Rafael Alberti and Jorge Guillén, the film director Luis Buñuel and, for 10 years, the artist Salvador Dalí. The poet Antonio Machado died of pneumonia while heading into exile in 1939. But the loss to Spanish cultural and intellectual life was even greater than this would suggest. Along with these giants there also went into exile, often for a lifetime, large numbers of university professors, lawyers, researchers, doctors and teachers. Francoism reshaped Spain not just politically and socially, but also intellectually.

The first experience of exile for most of the 400,000 refugees in France was as grim as anything they had endured during the war, or even worse. The reluctant French authorities provided at first no shelter, no medicine and almost no food. Refugees attempted to survive in what were essentially concentration camps on the windswept, winter coast, where they were prey to exposure, malnutrition and disease. Tens of thousands decided to risk returning to Spain. Those who did not, and who survived the conditions, gradually got better shelter, or found a way of moving away from the frontier and even, if they were lucky, getting passage on a boat to Mexico.

When the long-expected European war broke out in September 1939, thousands of Republican refugee soldiers enlisted in the French army or the French Foreign Legion, or labour battalions. For them, the war against fascism, lost in Spain, had recommenced. After the fall of France in 1940, this took the new form of participation in the French resistance against the German occupiers or their Vichy allies. But most Republican refugees were powerless against the German advance. Several thousand were transported to labour camps and concentration camps. Mauthausen and Oranienburg became part of the tragic itinerary that had begun in Madrid, or Barcelona, or any other of Spain's towns and villages in 1936.

The President of the Catalan Generalitat, Luis Companys, was handed back to Franco by the Nazis, and was executed. His fate was shared by other well-known Republican leaders. Former Prime Minister Francisco Largo Caballero managed to survive a German labour camp until the end of the Second World War, but then died of its effects. It was a peculiarly cruel end for a dedicated trade unionist who had striven to improve the working conditions of ordinary labouring men and women in Spain at the beginning of the Second Republic.

Rump Republican, Basque and Catalan governments all continued to exist in exile. Political parties that were banned in Spain also survived, after a fashion, in exile. In Spain itself, sporadic guerrilla operations against the regime irritated and occasionally troubled the authorities over several years. But the Spanish Civil War was over, and the Republic was utterly defeated, with its leaders killed, imprisoned or scattered, and its dreams destroyed.

The Spanish Civil War in perspective

On 15 March 1939, the German army invaded Czechoslovakia, just two weeks before the end of the Spanish Civil War. The Munich agreement of the previous September, which had ceded the German-speaking Sudetenland area of Czechoslovakia to Hitler, had not assuaged his appetite for territorial expansion. At a stroke, the Anglo-French policy of appeasement was undermined. It was now incontrovertible that Nazi ambitions went beyond the creation of a greater Reich of all German speakers, and extended, potentially without limit, across Europe.

The British and French governments issued a guarantee to Poland, demonstrating that their policy was now to deter German aggression, if necessary by war, rather than accommodate it. The scene was set for a European war, and the plot suddenly speeded up, with a new and ideologically bizarre twist, when the Nazi and Soviet governments agreed a non-aggression pact on 23 August. Safe in the knowledge that there would be no hostile reaction from the Soviet Union, Germany invaded Poland on 1 September. Two days later Britain and France honoured the guarantee they had issued, and declared war on Germany.

Europe was at war, but too late to affect the outcome of the Spanish Civil War. The convergence of the two conflicts that Negrín desperately hoped for had never happened. Spanish Republicans and the international volunteers who fought alongside them were doomed to have been 'premature anti-fascists', opposing Hitler and Mussolini in Spain before the western powers were prepared to confront them either there or anywhere else.

Consequences of the civil war

Measured against the scale of what would become the Second World War, the Spanish Civil War was a small affair. In the immediate context of Spain itself, however, a country of 24 million inhabitants, it was catastrophic. The Nationalist and Republican armies had swollen from the totals of about 70,000 soldiers, armed guards and initial volunteers each in mid-July 1936, to nearly one million men under arms on each side at the peak in 1938. About half a million people died in battle, behind the lines, and in the postwar repression. Many more were severely wounded, and the large number of people with missing limbs and other war wounds was a pitiful sight in Spain decades after the war ended. These *mutilados de guerra* or their children were given preferential access to jobs if they were Nationalists, but not if they had fought for the Republicans. If one adds to these the approximately 250,000 who went into permanent exile, it is evident that death, major disability and exile directly touched at least a million Spaniards, and indirectly very many more. Although these figures are estimates that may never be fully clarified, they are known to be approximately right, and the scale of the disaster they spell out is unmistakable.

Bereavement and grief were widespread. This was mitigated somewhat for Franco loyalists, whose dead and wounded were lauded as heroes. For Republicans, the despair experienced in defeat was exacerbated by the new regime's refusal ever to recognise that those who had died or been injured fighting against it were anything more than a rabble of crazed fanatics.

In economic terms, Spain was in a poor condition at the end of the war. Its finances were precarious. The Nationalists procured arms abroad worth about $700 million. A very large part of that total was still owed to Italy and Germany, whose willingness to provide military supplies on credit had made the Nationalist war effort possible. Franco was under strong pressure from Germany to make repayments swiftly during the Second World War in the form of exports of food and ores, and also by funding the Spanish Blue Division, which fought alongside the Germans on the Eastern Front. Debts to Italy were renegotiated downwards in May 1940, and payments of the reduced amount then continued until the 1960s.

The Republican campaign had also cost about $700 million for war material imported from abroad, but it had not generally relied on credit. In November 1936, when Negrín was Finance Minister in Largo Caballero's government, the gold reserves of the Bank of Spain were shipped to Moscow. They were converted into currency equivalents to pay the Soviet Union for the arms it supplied, and to buy arms elsewhere. By the end of the war, they were depleted.

In addition to these sums spent on arms procurement abroad by both sides, which in one way or another came out of Spanish resources, there were the huge internal costs of three years of fighting, including soldiers' pay, equipment and supply. Moreover, many houses and railway lines had been destroyed. Industry was hugely disrupted, though not badly damaged. Animal herds had declined by a third from prewar levels. In general, industrial and agricultural production was down by about a quarter in 1939, in comparison with 10 years' earlier. Per capita income had similarly dropped. It is not surprising that the 1940s are remembered in Spain as a miserable decade of privation.

Postwar austerity did not hit everyone equally hard. The Franco regime restored the great estates to their traditional owners. It was tolerant of black market profiteers. It pursued policies of autarky, which favoured domestic producers but created high prices for consumers. Life was particularly grim for the working classes and landless peasants, whose earlier hopes of escaping poverty had fuelled the Republican experiment of 1931, then the revolution of 1936–37. The new regime was certainly not going to make the interests and miseries of social groups it

regarded as godless *rojos* a priority. On the contrary, in a country with virtually no social security system, illness and unemployment spelt family ruin. Even for the millions in work, low wages and high prices made daily existence a struggle, and there was no independent trade union or left-wing party to care or to protest.

Franco completely dismantled Catalan and Basque autonomy, and suppressed the use of the Catalan, Basque and Galician languages, insisting that in all public spheres people should speak the language of empire, Spanish. All power was concentrated in Madrid. Postwar Spain was a society of the victors and the vanquished; there was no attempt at reconciliation. The Catholic Church enjoyed a degree of state support that was much greater than at any time since the 18th century. Government and church combined to preach order, hierarchy and discipline. The counter-revolution had triumphed.

Liberalisation and repression in postwar Spain

If Republicans and International Brigaders were premature anti-fascists, then the breakdown of the alliance of the United States and Britain with the Soviet Union after the Second World War made Franco into a premature Cold War warrior. He survived the Second World War and the eventual defeat of his Nazi and Fascist backers. He also survived the West's displeasure at the continuing existence of his dictatorship in the years immediately after 1945. Briefly, western ambassadors were withdrawn from Madrid. But by the end of the 1940s, the western powers were much too preoccupied by the Soviet threat as they perceived it, to worry unduly about the undemocratic Franco regime. In the new bipolar world, any anti-communist ruler had something to offer. In 1951 President Eisenhower agreed the first American grant to Franco, in exchange for the use of Spanish bases for the US air force.

Through the 1950s and 1960s Spain developed a powerful capitalist economy, with extensive industrialisation and an increasingly buoyant service sector. Other Europeans began to descend on it, not to fight in any ideological conflict, but to enjoy its sunny beaches in a new mass tourism. Living standards improved as the postwar years were left behind. Francoism presented the interesting paradox of economic liberalisation combined with repressive politics. When Franco died in November 1975, nearly 40 years after he took up arms against the Republic, Spain was still a dictatorship, but its economy and society had modernised.

To almost everyone's surprise, the institutions of the Franco regime were swiftly and peacefully dismantled from within after his death, in one of the most successful transitions from dictatorship to democracy of the late 20th century. King Juan Carlos was Franco's successor as head of state, and the grandson of Alfonso XIII, who had left Spain for exile in 1931 as the Second Republic was proclaimed. Unlike both of these predecessors, he proved to be a democrat. As early as 1978, the country enjoyed a new constitution, which defined Spain as a constitutional monarchy, based on popular sovereignty and democratic consultation, with autonomous regional communities, and without any state religion. Spain entered NATO in 1982, and the European Economic Community in 1986.

The Spanish Civil War in perspective

In retrospect, it sometimes became difficult to remember why the Spanish Civil War had been fought at all. Francoists had assumed for decades after the war that Spain would remain what they had made it – Catholic, authoritarian, nationalist and centralist. They suddenly found themselves living in a society full of the features they had sought to eradicate. It was now pluralist, tolerant, federal and multilingual. Militarism disappeared. Instead of the Second Republic being an anomalous period of democratic experiment, it seemed as though the long Franco regime was now the anomaly, separating two devolutionary democracies.

Things were no clearer to anti-Francoists. Democracy had somehow grown out of the dictatorship itself. There was continuity of economic growth and social transformation. Anarchism had disappeared. Nobody was a revolutionary any more. It was also obvious by the 1980s that the Spanish Communist Party was not a great force to be reckoned with. Everyone was a democrat. In what was soon labelled *el gran olvido*, the great forgetting, Spanish Socialists and Liberals turned their attention away from the repressive past of the dictatorship, and before that the polarisation of the civil war, to concentrate on building a modern, tranquil, affluent society. No one wanted to dwell on the painful memory of a bitter civil conflict. The wilder dreams of both extremes – Fascist and Anarchist, reactionary and revolutionary – seemed very distant.

The Spanish Civil War, however, should certainly be remembered. It represented for many Spaniards and non-Spaniards then, as it still does now, the first great, heroic confrontation between fascism and democracy in Europe. In this interpretation, the Second Republic remains a great cause that was worth dying for. It is quite possible to hold this view, while simultaneously recognising the Republic's political failures between 1931 and 1936, and the horrendous violence of the social revolution that erupted within it after the military rising of July 1936. It is also possible to feel repugnance for the harsh excesses of the military rebels and their subsequent dictatorship, while also recognising the fear and indignation that inspired their rebellion.

The very complexity of the issues at stake in Spain in the 1930s is itself a warning against over-simplification now. Men and women were caught up in confusing, threatening circumstances. Class aspirations, cultural identities and political ideologies criss-crossed in complicated and sometimes bewildering patterns. There were two sides, but many angles. Indeed, there were many different wars being fought within the Spanish

Civil War. From the vantage-point of the early 21st century, the experience of defeat looks as tragic as it ever did, but perhaps the completeness of the victory seems less sure.

In more strictly military terms, the Civil War occupies a very interesting position in the history of war. At one extreme, cavalry charges still sometimes proved effective, as in the Nationalist attack north of Teruel in February 1938. On the other, the use of air power, and the vital importance of supremacy in the air, pointed directly to the technology of the Second World War. One of the reasons that the Civil War lasted as long as it did is that air superiority oscillated between the two sides several times. Dominance in the air, such as the Nationalists enjoyed in the northern campaigns of 1937, gave an overwhelming advantage, but neither side enjoyed it all the time, or in all parts of the country simultaneously.

The nearly 3,000 planes engaged in the Spanish Civil War set a quite new pattern, especially in the context of Europe in 1936, when the Nazis were just beginning to implement their rearmament programme seriously, and Britain, still before rearmament, could boast only about 1,500 planes in the Royal Air Force. In strategic terms, it is probably in relation to the use of air power that the Spanish Civil War can most usefully be described as a small-scale rehearsal for the Second World War. Any contemporary observer of the resilience of Madrid, or the indignation at the bombing of Guernica, might also have suspected that relying on bombardment from the air to break civilian morale was misguided.

Several of the battles in Spain were reminiscent of the stalemate confrontations on the western front in the Great War. In successive initiatives by both sides round Madrid, defence proved easier than attack, and many lives were lost in order to advance

'Communism brings hardship, hunger, and ruin'. A Nationalist poster. The Nationalists produced fewer propaganda posters than the Republicans, and of lower quality. Throughout the war, the Nationalists called Republicans 'Communists' or 'Reds', just as Republicans called Nationalists 'Fascists'. Both labels were over-simplifications. (Author's collection)

a forward line a short distance, only for it to be driven back again, once more with high casualties, to within a few miles of where it began. Even the great Republican offensive over the Ebro in the late summer of 1938 petered out, and then turned into a determined resistance to the Nationalist counter-attack. The attack and counter-attack left both sides exhausted, yet the actual amount of territory in contention was small.

This pattern was also clear on a minor scale throughout the war in several battles for particular bits of high ground, as fighting to control or hold a particular hill, quite insignificant in peacetime conditions, claimed lives, limbs, and precious equipment. By the end of the war, many hills in Spain had been given the name 'Suicide Hill' by despairing soldiers. It is also true that the patterns of fighting changed during the war, as the militarily naive, urban volunteers for the Republic in 1936 learned that it was useless to brave artillery fire without protection, and accepted the need to dig trenches and think defensively.

On the other hand, there were some spectacular breakthroughs and rapid advances, most dramatically with the Nationalist attacking campaign into Catalonia in the winter of 1938–39, when defensive lines were pierced and the front virtually collapsed. In other battles, the use of tanks, artillery and air bombardment to prepare an advance were not yet *blitzkrieg*, but pointed towards it. The technology of war was visibly changing. Lessons were learned.

For a while in the 1930s, Spain seemed the centre of the world, the place where the great issues of the time were being decided. Most of the British volunteers who went to fight there were working-class men, often Communists, and usually already involved in class politics at home. Other pro-Republicans contributed medical knowledge, or money, to the Aid Spain campaign. Doctors, nurses, ambulance drivers and secretaries went to Spain to support the Republic and care for the wounded.

Writers, journalists and photographers were drawn to it as well, and it has often been through their eyes that the war has subsequently been viewed. Stephen Spender, W.H. Auden and Ernest Hemingway all went to Spain, and depicted the civil war as essentially an anti-fascist struggle. George Orwell, in *Homage to Catalonia*, analysed the divisions within the Republic from an anti-communist, pro-revolutionary perspective that was the basis more recently for Ken Loach's film *Land and Freedom*. The young British poets John Cornford and Julian Bell died in the fighting, and became symbols of the generous international idealism that drew so many to costly involvement.

Robert Capa's famous photograph of a lone Republican soldier being flung back by the force of a bullet at the very moment of death in August 1936 was published in major papers in several countries, and became the single most abiding image of the war. There has long been controversy over whether it was genuine or staged, with opinion moving recently rather more towards the conclusion that it was genuine. But whether accurate or not, it conveyed the central pro-Republican understanding of the war as a heroic struggle of ordinary, vulnerable, people against the military might of the rebel generals and their international backers.

In Spain itself after the war, the victors controlled the way it was depicted. In the regime's version of history, heroic Nationalists saved Spain from a rabble of murderous men and women, deceived by wild dreams of a classless Utopia. Until the 1960s, when censorship was somewhat liberalised, the regime even continued to claim that Guernica had been destroyed in a scorched-earth policy by the Republicans, rather than being bombed by the German air force. The dictatorship's constant propaganda and suppression of information made truth another casualty of the war.

It was for this reason that Hugh Thomas's monumental *The Spanish Civil War*, published in 1961, was such an important book. For the first time, a comprehensive account of what actually happened during the war existed, and although the Franco regime banned it, copies circulated widely in Spain. Forty years of subsequent scholarship have enormously enlarged our knowledge not just of the military course of the war, but more particularly of the politics, culture, economy and daily experience of the 24 million Spaniards whose fate it was to endure the conflict. The passage of time has not made the choices they faced seem any easier, or their courage any less remarkable.

Further reading

Alexander, W., *British Volunteers for Liberty*, London 1982.

Alpert, M., *An International History of the Spanish Civil War*, Basingstoke 1994.

Beevor, A., *The Spanish Civil War*, London 1982.

Buchanan, T., *Britain and the Spanish Civil War*, Cambridge 1997.

Fraser, R., *Blood of Spain*, London 1979.

Howson, G., *Arms for Spain: The Untold Story of the Spanish Civil War*, London 1998.

Nash, M., *Defying Male Civilization: Women in the Spanish Civil War*, Colorado 1995.

Preston, P., *Comrades: Portraits from the Spanish Civil War*, London 1999.

Thomas, H., *The Spanish Civil War*, 3rd edn, London 1977.

Index

Figures in **bold** refer to illustrations

agriculture 13, 18, 20-1, 69
Aguirre, José Antonio 52, 58
air force, Spanish 27, 30, **31**
aircraft 30, **31**, 91
  French 37-8
  German 40, 47, 54, **56**, 57
  Italian 40
  Soviet 46, 47, 49
Alcalá-Zamora, Niceto 18, 19, 20, 21, 22, 24
Alfonso XIII, king of Spain 13, 15, **15**, 89
Almendralejo 41
Anarchists
  in Civil War 36-7, 44, 47, 56-7, 58, 75, 82
  and Communists 8, 77
  ideas 8, 19
  and revolution 8, 22
  and unions 19, 20-1
Aragón, Council of 58, 68
Aranda, Col. Antonio 29
army, Spanish 17, 19, 24, 25-30
  see also Army of Africa
Army of Africa 30, **39**, 40-3, 47, 48, 65
Asensio, Gen. 50, 75
Assault Guards 25-6, 29, 30, 65
Asturias 22, 58
atrocities 41, 48, 72-5
Azaña, Manuel 18, **18**, 19, 20, 22, 24, 25, 27, 44, 64

Badajoz 24, 29, 41
Barcelona **14**
  and Anarchists 19
  in Civil War 33-5, 55-6, 64, 68, 69, 80
  living conditions 13, 80
  and military coup 27, **28**, 29
Basques 17, 25, 29, 51-2, 52-8, 68
  see also Catalonia; Vizcaya campaign
Belchite 58, 61
Bell, Julian 92
Berenguer, Sara 80-3
Bilbao 13, 27, 52-5, **54**
Bolín, Luís 26, 38
bombing 49, 53, 54, **58**, 72, **73**
Bosch, Gen. José 29
Britain 8, 10, 38, 45, 64, 87
  British volunteers 67, 91, 92
Browne, Felicia 70
Brunete 56-8, **57**
Burgos 45, 68

Cabanellas, Gen. Miguel 45, 68
Calvo Sotelo, José 25-6
Capa, Robert 92
Carlism and Carlists 8, 19, 22, 23, 36, 55, 65, 66, 83
Carod, Saturnino 66
Casado, Col. Segismundo 84
Casares Quiroga, Santiago 24, 27
Casas Viejas 20-1
Castelló, Gen. Luis 29, 37
Castilblanco 20
casualties 87
Catalonia 17, 18, 20, 22
  autonomous government of 29, 44, 68

Catholic Church
  and Basques 52
  and Nationalism 8, 41, 43, 55, 66, 69, 70, 83
  and Republicanism 17, 19, 20, 21, 24, 29, 72, 80
Cavalcanti, Gen. **45**
CEDA (Spanish Confederation of Autonomous
    Right-Wing Groups) 20, 21, 23, 24
Civil Guards 13, **14**, 19, 20-1, 29, 30, 65
CNT 19, 24, 66, 67, 75, 82
collectivisation 69
Comintern 46, 75
Communism and Communists 22, 77, **90**
  see also Anarchists; PCE; POUM
Companys, Luis 29, 86
Cornford, John 92

Dali, Salvador 86
Dávila, Gen. Fidel 55, 58
Durán, José 65-6
Durango 54
Durruti, Buenaventura 35, 49

Ebro, battle of the (1938) 61-4, **62**, **64**, 91
education 13, 18, 24, 71, 79
elections 13-15, 19, 21, 23-4
equipment 65, 67
Euzkadi 52-8, 68
exiles see refugees and exiles
Extremadura 41

Falange 8, 21-2, 24-5, 27, 36, 43, 55, 65, 72
Fanjul, Gen. 25, 27-9
fascism in Spain 68-9
  see also Falange
Faupel, Gen. Wilhelm **53**
fighting techniques 60, 91
FNTT (National Federation of Landworkers) 20, 21, 24
food supplies 65, 69
Foreign Legion, Spanish 22, 30, 40-3, **42**, 65
France 8, 10, 37-8, 45, 61, 64, 86, 87
Franco, Gen. Francisco **43**, **45**, **48**, **52**, **53**, **85**
  character 41, 43, 50
  conduct of Civil War 40-3, 49, 58, 63
  death and burial 85, 89
  foreign support 31, 38-40, 42, 53
  rise to and consolidation of power 22, 25, 26, 27,
    45, 55, 64, 68
  rule 7, 8, 54, 69-70, 84-6, 88-9
Fraser, Ronald 66
Free Women 71, 82

Gandesa 61, 63
García Escámez, Col. 36
García Lorca, Federico 72
Germany, support for Franco 7, 10, 31, 40, 42, 43, 45,
    47, 53, 54, 57
Gil Robles, José Maria 20, 21, 22, 23, 24, 25
Giral, José 27, 37, 44
Goded, Gen. 25, 29
Granada 29
Guadalajara, battle of (1937) 50-1
Guadalupe 41
Guadarrama hills 33, 36, **36**
Guernica **53**, 54, 72

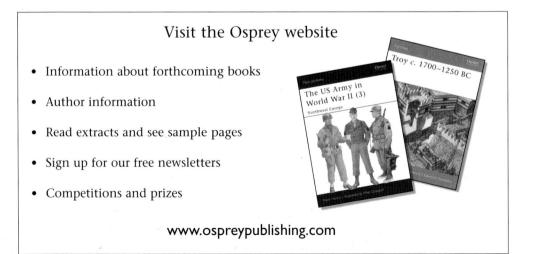